**LANGUAGE IN EDUCATIO**

Theory and Practice

**57**

# USING COMPUTERS
# in TEACHING
# FOREIGN LANGUAGES

# USING COMPUTERS
# FOREIGN

A publication of

 Center for Applied Linguistics

Prepared by

 ® Clearinghouse on Languages and Linguistics

# in TEACHING LANGUAGES

Geoffrey R. Hope

Heimy F. Taylor

James P. Pusack

 **HARCOURT BRACE JOVANOVICH, INC.**
Orlando    San Diego    New York
Toronto    London    Sydney    Tokyo

# LANGUAGE IN EDUCATION: Theory and Practice 57

This publication was prepared with funding from the National Institute of Education, U.S. Department of Education under contract no. 400-82-0009. The opinions expressed in this report do not necessarily reflect the positions or policies of NIE or ED.

Printed in the United States

ISBN   0-15-599306-2

# Language in Education: Theory and Practice

ERIC (Educational Resources Information Center) is a nationwide network of information centers, each responsible for a given educational level or field of study. ERIC is supported by the National Institute of Education of the U.S. Department of Education. The basic objective of ERIC is to make current developments in educational research, instruction, and personnel preparation more readily accessible to educators and members of related professions.

ERIC/CLL. The ERIC Clearinghouse on Languages and Linguistics (ERIC/CLL), one of the specialized clearinghouses in the ERIC system, is operated by the Center for Applied Linguistics. ERIC/CLL is specifically responsible for the collection and dissemination of information in the general area of research and application in languages, linguistics, and language teaching and learning.

LANGUAGE IN EDUCATION: THEORY AND PRACTICE. In addition to processing information, ERIC/CLL is also involved in information synthesis and analysis. The Clearinghouse commissions recognized authorities in languages and linguistics to write analyses of the current issues in their areas of specialty. The resultant documents, intended for use by educators and researchers, are published under the title Language in Education: Theory and Practice. The series includes practical guides for classroom teachers and extensive state-of-the-art papers.

This publication may be purchased directly from Harcourt Brace Jovanovich International. It also has been announced in the ERIC monthly abstract journal <u>Resources in Education</u> (<u>RIE</u>) and is available from the ERIC Document Reproduction Service, Computer Microfilm International Corporation, 3900 Wheeler Avenue, Alexandria, Virginia 22304. See <u>RIE</u> for ordering information and ED number.

For further information on the ERIC system, ERIC/CLL, and Center/Clearinghouse publications, write to ERIC Clearinghouse on Languages and Linguistics, Center for Applied Linguistics, 3520 Prospect Street, N.W., Washington, D.C. 20007.

*Sophia Behrens, editor, Language in Education*

# Contents

# I
# Fundamentals

## INTRODUCTION

In light of its progress over the past few decades, the computer seems to stand virtually outside of any reliable historical framework and suggests instead the world of fantasy: <u>Scientific American</u> reminds us that if the airplane had known comparable advances in technology, a 767 would now cost around $500 and "circle the globe in 20 minutes on five gallons of fuel" (Toong and Gupta 1982). Most foreign language teachers would know how to take advantage of such a development, though most of us would probably still require the services of an airline, if only to supply the pilots. The computer is different. It won't take us to Bogota, but it will fit in our classrooms; many language teachers are now asking where the pilots are. They earnestly want to investigate how the computer can serve them in the classroom.

The computer will continue to evolve, of course. Computer technology manages to challenge history paradoxically by creating a situation of constant change: there seems to be no secure vantage point in the present or past from which to take stock. This encourages people to dwell on futuristic notions of robot-like servants who may replace language students and teachers alike. At the risk of sticking in the mud, we want to keep our sights on the practical. We have resisted the temptation to reflect on a time when the computer may be able to judge and react to our emotional states at the keyboard, explain why an

1

unknown Czech author received the Nobel prize, tell
us the latest political joke from Bonn, compare notes
on our mutual acquaintances in Venezuela, or sing
passable soprano in a madrigal group.

What is practical and what exists, however, are
two separate realms. Right now, very little foreign
language computer material is on the market, and much
of what is available seems to be of little value.
Trivial games on expensive machines can do little to
accelerate our students' learning of language and
culture. We set out here to make and justify a
modest claim: the computer can be a useful, challenging, creative tool and resource in and around the
foreign language classroom. Like the blackboard, the
computer can be a serious and imaginative part of
classroom life to the extent that the teacher makes
it so.

Our audience is the foreign language instructor,
not simply as potential user and manager of
**computer-assisted instruction** (CAI), but also as
potential creator of computer lessons--a CAI author.
Do not panic: "CAI author" is a term that covers a
wide range of meanings. The instructor who types
twenty words at the keyboard of a computer in order
to have the machine produce a crossword puzzle is, in
a sense, a CAI author. To use the machine well, the
instructor must learn to control it in a number of
different ways that have little to do with jumping on
this year's bandwagon. Taking control requires easy
and constant access to the computer and the
opportunity to experiment to see what the computer
can, cannot yet, and never will be able to do. If
the machine is used but not made a personal, meaningful, and active part of the curriculum, it will
presumably come to be a waste of money, recalling
nothing so much as the tape-based language laboratory
and its historical misadventures.

We hope to avoid computer jargon and
mystification. Our impression, however, is that
oversimplification can mystify the curious language
teacher just as much as too much technical detail
can. When a term from the field of CAI first appears
in a chapter, we introduce it in **boldface** type.
These terms are explained in a glossary at the end of

the volume.

For much of our audience, computers are a new and highly technical subject.  For this reason, the issues of which equipment to use and how to acquire programs are not addressed until Chapter VI, "ACCESS TO CAI," following our discussion of the teaching tasks computers can handle.  In the interest of readability, we make very few bibliographic references in the body of the text; the annotated bibliography will serve to illustrate specific projects and to stimulate reading of research in the field.  The bibliography also includes several books and articles that list and evaluate commercially available programs--a task we have not undertaken here.

## ATTRACTIONS AND HURDLES

Students tend to be attracted to the computer. They may or may not learn significantly better with a computer than without one, but it is clear across the curriculum that they often enjoy the experience. Some of the efforts to enhance CAI with bells, visuals, and chummy remarks seem to miss the point: a well-designed foreign language lesson on the computer can be motivating in and of itself.

Many of the positive feelings CAI frequently engenders can be traced to a single factor:  the computer's liveliness.  While the screen may present nothing more in terms of content than a workbook does, by having each item pop up as though from nowhere, and by responding in some way to the student's answer, the **program** transforms otherwise inert exercises into active material.  Language study is particularly well suited to a dynamic context like this; some of the mind-numbing effects of written language exercises are changed into lively and engaging qualities by the computer.

The computer allows one-to-one interaction.  The amount of control over events is shared fairly equally between student and machine:  the computer asks the questions and has the answers; the student decides when to turn it on and off, which material to work on, and how fast to go. Students rarely have such power over their teachers. Teachers rarely seem as patient.

Personalized attention to detail is one of the computer's clearest benefits, but some programs also lend themselves to small-group work. STORYBOARD (Jones 1982) is a kind of **problem-solving** lesson in which students guess the words that will fill in a set of dashes, gradually causing a text to take shape. This program can be used by a single student, yet it can also foster a good deal of group excitement as students work together.

Besides being lively and intriguing, the computer shares another quality with good teachers: it keeps careful records and performs routine correction tasks. The arithmetic burden imposed on language teachers by their daily routine can be enormous. The computer can reduce the burden so that it seems almost bearable.

What stands in the way of putting this potential to best use? We find it difficult to imagine an area of the teaching profession that raises as many expectations as CAI, yet places as many hurdles between the teacher and the fulfillment of those expectations. Progress in the use of this technology is held back both by lack of access to equipment and by the need to develop a body of experience and knowledge in the use of computers. No other teaching technology purports to put a practical tool directly into our hands, yet requires such an investment of time to learn how to use. The general mystique surrounding computers and inflated notions about what they can do only add to the frustration. Anyone setting out to consider the use of computers in language teaching should be aware of the hurdles.

Access to equipment is a question of funds and policies. The relatively low cost of **microcomputing** has put computers on our doorsteps, yet sufficient equipment of the right type at the right time is seldom available to language teachers just beginning to explore possibilities. A familiar lament in the schools is that math and science teachers feel that a school's computers are their own property. The prospect of hordes of language students descending on their computers is not usually appealing. Another kind of equipment problem arises in the attempt to select computers appropriate to language teaching, or to make the available equipment somehow work for the kinds of programs one envisions. Chapter VI takes up the major equipment questions.

The greater hurdle, over the long term, is the need to know enough about using computers to make intelligent decisions. This does not always mean learning to write computer programs, but it does require becoming comfortable with developments in the field. Publications and workshops will contribute a great deal, but there is no substitute for teachers' willingness to experiment with available machines and programs. They can look forward to more than a few trying moments when they don't know what to do next, and the computer doesn't either. If they cannot consult support staff knowledgeable about computers, their own students may be the best resource. After making some strides, they may find it necessary to orient other faculty and administrators to what can be accomplished. Skepticism about the "inhuman" nature of computers readily yields to a healthy curiosity about the power of these machines to tackle our daily tasks and reduce our work load. The language-teaching profession, in fact, seems to be at the forefront among the disciplines of the humanities in exploring this technology. Nevertheless, teachers should expect serious questions about the relationship between the cost of the equipment and its putative benefits.

Teachers may encounter problems gaining regular access to equipment unless they have demonstrably good computer lessons in hand. It is difficult, however, to generate or evaluate computer materials without at least one readily available computer. This is a vicious circle that can be broken only with determination and imagination.

# BRIEF HISTORY

Thirty years ago, computers were as big as houses. Teams of experts were required to keep them going, and they were extremely expensive to use and to buy. Today, people in all walks of life use **microcomputers,** which are marketed as personal and home computers. The machines fit on desk tops and are relatively low priced; many serious questions about how to program them can be answered by high school students. The involvement of computers in our daily lives has become an established fact.

Since microcomputers have become so readily available, schools and colleges are using them on a regular basis. In the last three years, the number of microcomputers available to students in elementary and secondary education has increased significantly. It is estimated that three-fifths of all secondary schools have at least one microcomputer. This number will continue to rise in the next few years. More and more teacher-training programs have **computer literacy** as a basic objective: teachers are expected to be familiar with computers and deal easily with them.

Until recently, when microcomputers became available, students accomplished their CAI work on terminals that worked on large **mainframe** or **timesharing** computers. One large computer can support work at dozens of terminals simultaneously and has virtually unlimited space to store records and make computations of all kinds. Despite isolated successes with the use of large computers as so-called teaching machines, the future of computers in education, particularly outside the university setting, rests on the increased use of microcomputers. In many areas of **instructional computing,** microcomputers outstrip the large computers and terminals typically available to students at colleges and universities. In any case, these distinctions are rapidly becoming irrelevant as technological change makes it possible to pack more and more power into the tiniest devices.

I. FUNDAMENTALS

Perhaps more important than the number of terminals or microcomputers at an institution is the availability of computer programs or **software**. The potential of CAI in education has been demonstrated in hundreds of programs created in the last decade. Some of them are good; some of them are not. A major drawback of programs, even when they do prove successful, is the question of **compatibility**. Computers do not all speak the same language; language teachers will understand better than others when they learn that computers have mutually incomprehensible dialects. Instructional materials, known as **courseware**, that have been developed for one brand of machine will seldom work on another. Good microcomputer programs may use all the bells and whistles of their machine to accomplish their tasks, but manufacturers seldom agree with each other on which bell or which whistle should be built into their products. Many teachers interested in CAI have consequently had to create their own programs that will work on their own computers.

Another factor that drives instructors to write their own materials has been the lack of commercially available programs with applications for foreign language teaching. This dearth of courseware is somewhat puzzling, since many principles of language pedagogy, such as flexibility, individualization, accuracy in detail, and rapidity of response, are fundamental advantages of teaching with computers.

The earliest large-scale projects--in the 1960s--were the German program at the State University of New York at Stony Brook and the Russian program at Stanford University. Tremendous efforts were expended at both institutions and valuable lessons were learned, but cost, problems of integrating computer-based materials into the curriculum, and the difficulties of sharing courseware with other institutions kept these and other early projects from having a significant impact on the profession.

Other institutions, among them Dartmouth; the Ohio State University; and the universities of Minnesota, Illinois, Iowa, and Alberta, developed their own programs in foreign languages. Some of these projects enjoyed substantial support from private industry; others resulted from the unheralded toil of individual faculty members. The PLATO system at Illinois received nationwide attention and today offers programs in a number of foreign languages and English as a second language. Ohio State's German programs--TUCO (Tutorial Computer) and DECU (Deutscher Computerunterricht)--are **tutorial** in nature and contain first-year elementary grammar explanations and exercises. They were developed in 1973/74 and are still used by several hundred students each year at Ohio State and other institutions. Systems such as PLATO and FRAND, used at Alberta, utilize not only computer terminals with normal typewriter keyboards, but also audio devices and touch-sensitive screens on which students can point to their answers rather than type them.

Many other institutions developed their own CAI projects in the seventies; most were tailor-made for local language programs. Objectives depended on **hardware** facilities, financial support, interest of individuals in language or computer departments, and the expertise of those who were creating the computer programs. Almost all these programs used mainframe computers and served as adjuncts to regular classroom instruction.

Although numerous CAI programs were developed for foreign languages in the late sixties and early seventies, widespread implementation of CAI did not take place. Several problems have persisted over the years. Until recently, language teachers often exhibited skepticism toward the ever-changing technology of computers. Myths prevailed, including the notion that one had to understand the mechanics of these machines in order to be able to use them. The reluctance of the profession to accept CAI as a tool in language instruction was frequently caused by fear that computers would replace teachers. This fear has proved to be totally unwarranted. It tends to linger, however, as one namable fear in the face of many unnamable fears engendered by the computer's novelty, omnipresence, and power.

Very few language teachers were willing to participate in the development of software, particularly since administrative and academic

recognition of such efforts was slow to come. A
general lack of computing skills among foreign
language teachers often consigned the writing of
software to computer experts who had little knowledge
of foreign languages or how to teach them. Where the
contribution of language teachers was minimal, the
software was not very effective. The remarkable
capabilities of computers were of very little value
when programs did not reflect sound pedagogy.

Among the biggest stumbling blocks along
teachers' paths toward adopting CAI were the high
initial cost of hardware and program development and
the poor quality of the programs themselves. As
Holmes and Kidd (1982) have explained, problems arose
from the delicate nature of the machinery, reduced
industry financing, inconclusive empirical evidence
concerning the effectiveness of CAI, and the impression that many CAI programs merely duplicated
instruction that could be performed better and
usually more cheaply by other means. These factors
have contributed to the lack of enthusiasm and support for many projects.

In 1980, Olsen published the results of her survey on the use of CAI in 1,810 foreign language
departments. She concluded that though there was
enthusiasm for CAI, it was rather limited. Negative
attitudes were expressed largely because of high
cost, lack of facilities for diacritical marks, scar-
city of ready-made computer programs, and the absence
of skilled personnel. At the time of her survey,
most of the respondents were using mainframe computers. Although the cost of time-sharing systems
such as PLATO has been steadily reduced, the price
per instructional hour remains relatively high.
Olsen indicated, however, that a number of respondents expressed optimism and enthusiasm regarding the
potential of microcomputers, which were just beginning to enter the educational market at the time of
her research.

A major problem facing CAI right now is the
haphazard way information has been disseminated
regarding existing computer programs and those under
development. Good programs, including some recently
developed for microcomputers, have not been publicly

documented in such a way that others can learn from them. Only a few programs are commercially available, and numerous teacher/programmers are working independently, often having little or no knowledge of existing programs or those being developed. At professional meetings, it is not unusual to see demonstrations of simple programs that are well behind the state of the art. Though these programs have little or nothing unique to offer, they frequently elicit a great deal of interest because the teaching profession remains largely ignorant of what can be expected in this field.

We urgently need more appropriate and pertinent programs to enhance students' learning and to lead us from the arena of "fun and games" into the realm of effective education. Some textbook companies are already producing software, but foreign language textbook publishers have resisted this trend and are just beginning to show an interest in the production and marketing of **software packages**. National organizations, such as CALICO (Computer-Assisted Language Learning and Instruction Consortium), formed at Brigham Young University in 1983, are attempting to assist in the production and evaluation of instructional materials. More powerful theoretical approaches to instructional uses of the computer are emerging. We hope that these efforts will be matched by those of the profession itself. Our journals should include reviews of software as legitimate teaching materials. We should be able to read reports by actual users and not simply the armchair opinion of the reviewer. Grants should support larger projects undertaken by teams of teachers, computer experts, and cognitive scientists.

Perhaps we can finally begin to exploit fully the powerful language-teaching resources that computer technology has made available. A note of caution is nevertheless in order. Technology must not dictate educational goals and methods. A clear understanding and sympathy for the principles of second language learning are much more important than computer expertise. Computer-assisted instruction will certainly fail unless it is designed and implemented by the people who have the central

interests of foreign language teaching at heart--the
teachers.


## HANDLING NATURAL LANGUAGE


The goal of using a machine to teach a foreign
language can be approached in many ways.  To the
extent that the subject matter resembles the teaching
of other bodies of facts and principles--history,
medicine, the sciences--the computer can offer a
dynamic way to present material and check on
students' progress.  When we attempt, however, to
simulate the experience of speaking a foreign
language via the computer, we encounter enormous
difficulties.  The computer has no built-in way to
understand natural language, which makes it difficult
to construct programs that contribute meaningfully to
the process of language learning.  It will be useful
to consider the problems of handling natural language
as a basis for more detailed discussion of the role
the computer can be expected to play in building
language skills.
Anyone just embarking on an exploration of what
computers can do for language teaching will soon be
astounded by the limited range of fundamental
operations most computers can perform.  The computer
languages built into most small computers have a
fairly versatile arsenal of techniques for handling
mathematical functions but a rather primitive set of
tools for handling verbal information.  Most machines
have operations that allow the program to compare two
expressions to see if they are the same, to assemble
words into sentences, or to recombine segments of a
short piece of text.  Some machines, though, even
lack a convenient way to scan a text to see if it
contains a given word or phrase.
The computer can certainly carry out complex
syntactic operations; such operations, however, are
exceedingly time consuming and may involve advanced
forms of programming.  Operations that might border
on **artificial intelligence**, such as the manipulation

of hierarchical lists, are not widely available on small computers, although this is changing. Small computers also lack the ability to draw immediately on large **databases**, such as lexicons and topic-related scripts or scenarios, which are essential for pseudo-conversational interaction. As teachers acquire computers that are more and more powerful, these limitations will disappear, but for the time being they affect the kinds of programs we can use with students.

Because of these constraints, the handling of natural language materials, especially those generated by students, is bound to remain at a frustratingly low level for the near future. Many programs available today make no attempt to analyze the forms and patterns of the students' typed answers. The few programs that do so have achieved this result either by using most of the resources of the machine or by dint of tedious effort that must be repeated for each lesson or program. There are currently no automated systems on any computer that can fully analyze the structure of freely created sentences. Research into these problems belongs to the field of artificial intelligence and is conducted using only the largest computers. Such research typically deals with well-formed utterances, not with the malformed sentences inevitably generated by our students.

For the purposes of CAI, the fully automated processing of freely created sentences is only a dream. In one fashion or another, language-teaching programs drastically reduce the range of valid sentences the student can produce, and thus simplify the computer's analytical task. Right/wrong and multiple-choice questions are common solutions that usually fail to satisfy most teachers. Short-answer drills are popular and can be quite effective, yet it should be understood that programs that manage to handle even the verb system of a single language strain the capacity of small computers. Although resourceful programmers will make strides, the problem of handling student errors will continue to hamstring our efforts to analyze natural language responses.

I.  FUNDAMENTALS

Today, foreign language instructional computer programs tend to resemble drills, rather than conversation. When our programs manage to simulate anything, it is frequently the classroom, not real life. We are struck by the apparent paradox that the most complex technology is being used to accomplish the most primitive pedagogical goals. What we face is not so much a dead end as a challenge to find the appropriate uses for the available technology. By combining high-quality, computer-based practice with imaginative uses of audio, video, and human interlocutors, we may be able to offer our students useful learning environments and temporarily side-step the issue of making computers "understand" natural language. At the same time, research into this more thorny area may well provide models for exciting instructional possibilities just over the horizon.

## INTERACTION AND COMMUNICATION

The teacher's most important and effective activity in the classroom is to interact with students. Personal contributions by students and instructor enhance class discussions, question-and-answer sessions, and even simple drill and practice lessons. When mistakes are made, good teachers not only give correct answers but also, through a process of verbal and nonverbal interaction, help students recognize their errors, analyze them, and come up with correct answers. This method of teaching and learning is more interesting and effective than passive methods where students are simply instructed or informed. Unfortunately, interaction techniques are difficult to use extensively with large groups of students and work best on a one-to-one basis or with only a few learners in a group. They can become very expensive because they require what are, for the most part, unrealistic teacher/student ratios. In most teaching situations, individualized interactions between teachers and students or among students are too few.

One of the most attractive features of the computer, then, is its ability to interact with students. Good computer programs make extensive interaction between computer and student possible. In the case of mainframe systems, a particular program can interact with a large number of students at the same time. When microcomputers are used, each student requires access to an individual computer. In either case, it is important to distinguish between interaction with a computer and human interaction. While the latter implies, even at a minimum, a rich network of meaningful communicative lines back and forth between individuals, the computer's interactive capabilities are simple and mechanical. To a large extent, we prefer to think of interaction between a student and computer, however extensively developed, as essentially noncommunicative. In good designs we may achieve the illusion of communication, and computers can certainly present information and test acquisition of skills and knowledge, but for our purposes, communicative activities are best thought of as remaining essentially human, cultural, personal, and unprogrammed.

The interaction that can take place between a program and its user ultimately depends on quite simple procedures. The program must obtain information from the student; this is called **polling** the student. The program must then use this information in some follow-up procedure. At the simple end of the spectrum, a program can present information to students and interact with them by showing the next **frame** when they press a key. This technique is very common in the presentation of instructions.

Once students have provided some information--an answer, a selection from a list of options--it must be evaluated. The procedure typically consists of operations either based on a simple yes/no decision (Was a valid letter typed at all? Has the correct answer been chosen?) or involving a more elaborate decision (How closely does the response match the correct answer? Is the first word correct? --Yes. Is the second word correct? --No.).

No matter how complex the decision made by the computer, it ultimately consists of a large number of smaller decisions, such as determining whether or not a memory area containing--in human terms--the word "cat" has a pattern of data identical to another space of interest to the program. If this other space contains information humans would decode as "dog," then the computer is really charged with deciding whether a pattern like:

010000110100000101010100

is the same as:

010001000100111101000111.

Bigger computers and smarter programs do not have better ways of doing this; they simply perform the most elementary operations faster and more efficiently. It is perhaps unnecessary to stress that the computer will never realize that what it internally calls a 010001000100111101000111 can bark.

Once the analysis of a response is accomplished, the program's next move may be simple (present the next item) or complex (register a wrong answer; show clues about the right answer; compute the percent wrong so far; determine how many items have been done at this point; present this kind of information to the student; suggest an alternate series of questions; and so on). In a simple true/false, multiple-choice, or fill-in-the-blanks exercise with little or nothing in the way of helpful commentary, interaction is kept to a minimum. However, in some tutorial programs, interaction can reach a sophisticated level. A description of useful interactive possibilities will be presented below. These include different kinds of **presentation** frameworks, **diagnosis, record keeping,** and **branching** decisions.

When various features of interaction between student responses and information displayed on the screen are combined, the computer can become less of a mechanical device and begin to "humanize" machine-based learning. Indeed, the goal of the most promising programs is to create environments where students produce the <u>questions</u>, rather than the <u>responses</u>.

Programmed imaginatively, the machine embodies the best strategies and insights of the experienced language teacher, multiplying the teacher's contacts with students for certain kinds of language practice. Good programs can offer, in this way, individualized attention and can allow students to work at their own pace. Students can work in privacy without fear of reprisal or ridicule regardless of how slow they might be or how often they give incorrect answers. Immediate diagnosis saves time and frustration and helps students weed out their errors. Computers possess the quality of infinite patience. They treat each student in the same way without favoritism. They are also very consistent in their responses, regardless of how many hours they have been working. Even the best of teachers cannot show the same level of enthusiasm, interest, and energy, day in and day out.

Though virtually tireless, computers can become tiresome. If a student gives a creative answer to a grammar exercise, a classroom teacher can respond appropriately, laugh or make an acknowledging gesture, and come up with a good rejoinder. This type of behavior encourages communication. The computer program typically searches for patterns and, finding none or few in an imaginative or witty response, produces a standard error message. This kind of behavior might discourage creative efforts. Teachers who hope to rely on the computer for much beyond the formal mechanisms of language may be neglecting the best communicative device possible: themselves and their classrooms. Computers should be used for what they can do best; by expecting too much from them, we risk creating more problems than we solve.

# TYPES OF CAI

We rely on a somewhat standardized taxonomy of interactive forms in CAI. Five terms are widely used to describe the way computer lessons in any field can be conducted: tutorials, drill and practice, problem solving, simulations, and games.

**Tutorial** lessons present new information to the student. They consist of explanations, rules, principles, charts, tables, definitions of terms, exercises, and appropriate branching. Weak tutorials are very much like textbooks; they are filled with what might be called instructional narrative. Strong tutorials break new concepts down into manageable pieces and check the student's comprehension frequently.

**Drill and practice** assumes that basic concepts have already been offered to the students, who can now proceed to apply rules, work with concrete cases, and explore their own grasp of the material. Drill is a fast-paced check on discrete points in the students' knowledge. Weak grammar drill aims at rote memorization of forms; strong drill challenges the students' grasp of principles and teaches through helpful correction of error.

**Problem solving** is practice on a higher plane than drill. Larger tasks involving several steps and processes are presented to the students, who use the computer as a tool or a resource in a quest for a solution. In good problem-solving programs, the computer keeps track of the students' approaches to the problem and analyzes their flaws.

**Simulations** are computer analogues of real-life situations into which students are catapulted for the purposes of reaching a global understanding of a process. Often, the underlying principles that determine the students' path are not made explicit, but must be deduced from several experiences of the simulation. Simulations may be used to practice a skill, such as learning to fly an airplane or drive a car, or to understand and appreciate systems in economics, ecology, anatomy, urban planning, and other disciplines.

**Games** are familiar enough from video arcades and need little explanation. Instructional games involve the mobilization of knowledge to overcome obstacles and reach goals. The obstacle can be the students' own imperfect knowledge; the goal can be achievement of subject-matter mastery. Weak games tend to associate the exercise of skills with situations and rewards extrinsic to the subject matter. Good games are well-disguised simulations.

In foreign language CAI, this typology quickly breaks down. Good tutorials involve extensive practice and "simulate" the classroom. Drill is often dismissed as mechanical or "Skinnerian," largely because weak programs offer the student little help in reaching a correct answer. Advanced types of structural practice probably should be classified as problem solving. Simulations may be little different from drill if they can handle only a small number of precise foreign language responses to a given situation; if they use multiple-choice questions, they may be better classified as reading exercises. While we use the traditional classification scheme, we recommend that it be viewed skeptically, especially when these terms are invoked in a judgmental fashion, in order to heap scorn upon drill, or to extol the glories of simulation. Good CAI materials in foreign languages seldom meet the challenges of the field in predictable ways.

# II

# Exploring
# the Landscape

## INVITATION

In order to show the relationship between the
goals of a language teacher and the practical steps
involved in using the computer as a teaching tool, a
relatively simple example is needed. We have chosen
what appears to be, at first glance, a rather humdrum
topic--the teaching of vocabulary--in order to
demonstrate in some detail the capabilities and
limitations of computers in foreign language
education. Our intent is to help our readers explore
the hills and valleys, even a cave or swamp, of the
computer landscape, without causing them to trip over
the roots and rocks of actual **programming**. We
invite them to take this short tour before going on
to our survey of issues in foreign language computing. Without such a guided tour, we feel our
remaining discussion might only befog the path.

Vocabulary is a good example for us, because
there is little agreement about how and if it should
actually be taught. In the face of grand theories of
contextual and communicative language learning, practical considerations lead most teachers, sooner or
later, to teach words out of context, even using the
native language, in order to give their students a
boost into some area of grammar or culture. The
example of vocabulary reflects the uneasy relationship between theory and practice that plagues our
field, especially when we try to adapt a flexible
teaching strategy to a machine-based interaction.

From the computer side of things, the topic of
vocabulary also suggests itself because it is one
area that seems destined to spawn so many bad pieces
of **software**.  Give a foreign language student a
computer, or try to teach a computer whiz kid a
foreign language, and two days later you'll have a
vocabulary drill program on your hands.  It will be a
so-called **flashcard program** that presents
**associated pairs** of native/target language words
dissociated from all reality:   see an English word,
type a German word; if you're wrong, you're wrong;
three tries and you're out.  Programs like this give
drills a bad name.  Fancier versions let students
build colorful pyramids or shoot down enemy space-
ships.  Strangest of all, teachers may even notice
substantial improvement in students' vocabulary after
they have obliterated several fleets of alien
invaders.

Keeping such programs in mind, let us explore
the way good teaching methods and computers can be
combined.  When we teach vocabulary, we are concerned
with the choice and classification of words, the manner of presentation, possible kinds of practice, and
methods of testing comprehension or mastery.  All
these related areas affect the ways in which teachers
can integrate computers into language study.

The computer seems to adapt particularly easily
to elementary vocabulary study, but teachers will
seldom have identical views about how many or which
words to teach or how vocabulary is best acquired and
retained.  The lexicon of a language is not nearly as
restricted or as systematic as are sounds and grammatical structures; this means vocabulary is a highly
variable element of the curriculum.  Textbooks
frequently fail to organize vocabulary items for
systematic presentation, practice, and review.
Vocabulary is personal.  While words may be presented
systematically, it is next to impossible for teachers
and textbook authors to decide which words must be
acquired for active use and which ones may continue
to be understood but not used.  The focus on communicative skills, usage, and proficiency levels does
not particularly encourage the study of vocabulary
per se.  The whole idea of dissecting language into

parts for analysis and practice can cause professional anxieties. It is clear that vocabulary cannot and should not be learned only through specific practice, but primarily by encountering words through listening and reading. In many spoken contexts, nothing can replace the fluent speaker as a source of the meaning and usage of words, and to read literature, a good dictionary will always be essential.

There is, despite these problems, a place in our curricula for specific work on vocabulary, just as there is room for practice with grammatical, phonological, and cultural systems that support communicative efforts. Computerized exercises can help students become familiar with significant amounts of vocabulary at the elementary and intermediate levels. The computer should contribute new ways of systematizing and conducting vocabulary study. This basic position should underlie the design of any effective computer lesson for language study.

## VOCABULARY FILES

Most of the power of a computer derives from its ability to compare many things very rapidly. Even a novice programmer will soon learn how to store lists of words, flash them on the screen, and compare student answers with right answers. These operations will form the basis for any vocabulary program. For use in a computerized lesson format, vocabulary is typically stored as **files**, which are simply lists of items set aside for use at the proper moment by the computer's program. The program knows what to do; the files are grist for its mill.

The computer program acts as a management system with a number of functions including the storage of information about the words and the different groups or categories they fill, a means of retrieving the words according to given categories, and a strategy for presenting them to the student. Frequently, there is a system to keep track of the actual use of

the words in lessons, particularly information on
right and wrong answers.

There are many ways to store vocabulary for use
in exercises. To give an idea of how the process may
work, we will look at the structure of a relatively
simple file and show how an elementary program could
use it. The file described can also be used to support any number of other exercise types, but word-to-
word correspondence is particularly common because it
is easy to use both in class and on the computer.

This kind of lesson can be dismissed both as a
trivial use of a complex machine and as a
pedagogically questionable way of teaching
vocabulary. Better vocabulary exercises use a more
secure and relevant context. Word-for-word translation does represent an easy means of access to teaching foreign languages through computers, however, and
remains a relatively sure way of walking through a
large number of words. The following is the kind of
exercise that teachers or their students can write
with very little programming experience.

The lesson asks students to indicate whether
they want to translate German words into English or
English words into German. Words are displayed on
the screen with a place for the student to put the
answer:

        der Arzt
    -->


The file is organized by topic--in this case, medical
professions. This is already a major step beyond the
run-of-the-mill vocabulary drill, which simply follows the miscellaneous sequence dictated by the
current textbook chapter. The topics can be subject-
matter groupings, as illustrated here, or more wide-
ranging notional or functional groupings. Even
though the words may pop up out of sentence context,
it seems reasonable to assume that the network of
associations generated by topic-related words will
form a useful context in itself as the drill progresses.

The precise way the words are stored by the computer is dictated by the logic of the program. The

programmer designs a simple format that will be handy for both the computer and the human being who must create the lesson files. In our case, the file consists of words in both languages linked by dashes:

die Krankenschwester--nurse
der Krankenpfleger--male nurse
der Arzt--doctor
etc.

This format allows the file to be used to construct a drill or to present words with their meanings, one pair at a time, as a glossary or "help" feature.

The program that employs this file can merely run down the list, picking words in a fixed sequence, or may choose words at random. Random selection, which may seem to contradict the logical nature of the computer, is itself a fascinating mechanism that has been built into even the simplest computers. By exploiting the ability to pick items at random or present them in a scrambled sequence, we can already move beyond paper-and-pencil drills to ever-varying forms and orders of a basically simple drill.

The lesson may terminate when all the words in the file have been used or when a specific group of words the student asks for has been presented. With just a bit more programming power and space, the program may keep track of missed words and intermingle them with new words as the drill proceeds. The weakest aspect, pedagogically, of most drill programs, is their failure to recycle missed items until they are mastered. Simple **optimizing** procedures, which require a student to meet a given level of mastery before **retiring** an item from the larger **pool,** harness the power of the computer to adjust the sequence of instructional events to the ability of the student. A well-designed program also should check to see whether a wrong answer (e.g., Spanish "pero" for "perro") is really the right answer to another item, indicating confusion between two items. If so, the two confused items should both be recycled until the student can distinguish between them properly.

When the computer presents a word to a student, it must display only one half of the pair in the file and ask the student to match the associated half. There is no magic to this at all: everything the program finds to the left of the dashes is in one language, everything to the right of the dashes is in the other. Programming this step involves using operations in the computer that scan the line of text for the dashes and that carve out the English and German pieces. One piece is displayed, and the other piece is used for comparison with the student's answer. If the two are identical, the program records a correct answer and moves on to the next item.

Now the program begins to get interesting. Any program can determine whether two **strings** (groups of characters) match or fail to match. A mismatch indicates an error. However, a teacher would not treat many mismatches as errors, while a primitive program would have to count them wrong. At this point, it becomes clear that good teaching principles must determine the fundamental design of the program. Judgments concerning the correctness or specific incorrectness of a response involve techniques known as **answer processing**. The crude flashcard program will simply say, "Wrong, try again." A sophisticated program will guide the student to a correct answer.

Even before such concerns are brought into play, however, miscellaneous typing problems should be accounted for. Did the student type too many spaces? add punctuation? engage the shift lock? Are these errors or typos? Good programs will not let trivial errors--errors that would not affect the quality of an answer--count as incorrect responses. An editing step is required to delete extraneous material and compensate for capitalization. On the other hand, a German teacher might insist that nouns be capitalized. The program must anticipate this eventuality, too.

In response to "der Arzt," a student might well write "physician" or "the doctor," neither of which would provide an exact match with the answer "doctor" from our file. Programs and file structures can be designed to handle multiple correct answers like

"physician" and "doctor" (with or without the
definite article). An easier way out of the problem
of alternate correct answers is to have students work
from a list, which may simply be a printed copy of
the file itself, to study the words needed for the
drill. By working with the list the student comes to
avoid using "physician" to translate "der Arzt." A
complex program requiring much time, money, and
effort to create may not produce results that are
significantly different from those achieved by a
relatively simple program. The choice between
elaborate analysis and simplified subject-matter
presentation is a issue of lesson design that only
language teachers can resolve.

A new level of complexity is introduced by the
likelihood that students will not simply arrive at
one of several correct answers, but will make various
kinds of errors. As long as the student types an
answer correctly, the computer can easily find it in
a list of possible right answers. But what happens
with answers like "phisician" or "docter" or something that looks like neither or a little like
either? Think of the Arab ESL student to whom "sgrt"
spells the English word for a tobacco product. Even
where reasonable misspellings are present, a good
program should be able to find both a way to guess
which alternative is intended and a way to focus
students' attention on the nature of their errors.
Various approaches and strategies are outlined below
in the discussion of grammar, where this task becomes
even more difficult.

Above and beyond the problems of spelling, good
programs will give systematic kinds of help to the
student in areas where rules and principles are being
taught. In vocabulary programs, gender errors can
give rise to diagnostic messages like "Watch out,
this is not a feminine noun." More elaborate clues
can be provided, like "Many German nouns ending in e
are feminine." Good programs will build these messages into the program logic. In the second case,
the program would check every German item in the
drill to see if it had "die" as the article and ended
with e. Here the computer begins to acquire
something akin to a rudimentary knowledge of the

foreign language; it is no longer merely comparing groups of characters. Extending this approach to full-sentence answers, however, boggles the mind of any programmer.

The preceding sketch of a simple vocabulary program should provide the reader with a feeling for the combination of simple operations that forms the nucleus of most instructional computer programs in foreign languages. The program handles structured information, presents it, and analyzes the performance of the student in helpful ways. Arriving at such a mechanism is neither the beginning nor the end of a project using computers in instruction. It is a small step in the middle of a larger process of instructional design that has much more to do with teaching than with computers. The remainder of this chapter deals with the kinds of design questions that should be tackled by teachers before they buy or write a computer program for any type of language study. Our discussion is intended to reflect the high proportion of solid language pedagogy, relative to technical questions, that is required for good CAI. In areas more complex than vocabulary study, this proportion can favor teaching concerns over programming tasks even more strongly.

## CHOICE OF WORDS

While it is conceivable that complete dictionaries may be stored for computer use, the more practical program will limit and control its focus. Programs designed for vocabulary practice should be based on a corpus that has some recognizable rationale. A number of considerations can help teachers write or choose computerized supplements for vocabulary study that are practical, flexible, and long lasting. At the elementary levels, the choice of words to put into computer exercises should clearly be made on the basis of modified frequency lists. Standard references listing the most common and useful elementary words, expressions, verbal functions, and the means of classifying them, should occupy an important place in the construction of vocabulary units. Some programs, of course, will present words from commercial textbooks, following the sequence of chapters and associated with the relevant grammar. Systematic lists of words can be supplemented both by personal lists compiled by teachers or students and by words from specific readings.

Most professional sources agree that little vocabulary should be presented at the first level, when students are encountering a new system of sounds and grammar. In later stages, as students master structures, more and more words can be added, with more subtle discrimination of meanings. On the other hand, elementary students who control a relatively large corpus of content words can avoid the feeling that they must communicate at infantile levels. A few simple structures (e.g., "I like . . ." or "I hate . . .") can support a good deal of content and perhaps increase motivation. Flexible computer programs that integrate words into meaningful situations should be able to facilitate the rapid rehearsal and eventual acquisition of large amounts of vocabulary.

The effort to determine the number of words students should, can, or do learn is probably most meaningful when undertaken with individual learners or classes in view. Teachers whose classes have easy access to computerized vocabulary exercises should be able to judge for themselves the amount of vocabulary their students seem to be acquiring at different levels. In order to form an accurate impression of how many words students are learning, teachers must have vocabulary programs at their disposal that can manage several thousand words in meaningful categories. The program should recirculate vocabulary in different contexts and maintain records of student performance from session to session.

Flexible programs will allow students to choose the number of words they would like to study. Groups of about twenty words provide the requisite amount of mutual distraction while allowing for fairly rapid recycling and progress through the pool. It should be easier for students to judge their own progress through lessons of this length than through lessons of fifty or sixty items. At any rate, lessons should be varied, and mastery of a word in one context should not be taken to mean that it has been mastered for good.

## CLASSIFICATION OF WORDS

Grouping vocabulary is thought to aid retention, so vocabulary files should allow for as many different groupings as possible. Good students apparently learn by making their own groups of words. This can be possible with a program that allows students to build their own files. For each student a program can also make a personal file of words missed, in order to recirculate them.

Vocabulary lessons typically consist of words and expressions grouped and presented in one of five major ways, each of which can be valuable both in the presentation of words for teaching purposes and for exercises requiring some sort of response. Vocabulary programs on the computer can use all five types, drawing on the same words and expressions in various modes of presentation. Large, well-structured programs with hundreds or thousands of words will assign each word to several groups simultaneously. Smaller programs can simply work with lists that consist of words all grouped in one of the following ways.

In the curriculum based on grammar, words are classified according to part of speech. While prepositions, conjunctions, pronouns, and interjections are not normally treated as vocabulary, nouns, verbs, adjectives, and many adverbs are. A system that can retrieve words in these categories can be put to use for both grammar and vocabulary exercises.

The most familiar of the ways of grouping vocabulary is the content area list. These often consist of nouns and include areas such as foods, body parts, animals, the home, travel, or art. These

lists can be useful in establishing an overall
familiarity with a topic and are good sources for
technical vocabulary (e.g., names of wildflowers or
banking terms), but they can easily remain artificial, divorced from meaningful use. They are
sometimes more satisfactory when meanings and
relationships are established by pictures rather than
by native equivalents. The use of images, rather
than text, as the basis for vocabulary drill is
discussed below. Exercises with content lists can be
"open": the student is invited to list six parts of
a car. The program searches the relevant file to
find a match with each answer as the student types
it. This format allows a kind of freedom for the
student and may work best with a visual image shown
either on the screen or in the form of a handout. A
"closed" exercise with a similar list could have the
student identify one of five words that does not
belong with the others. The program presents four
words at random from one file group and one word at
random from another.

Exercises that work from <u>functional</u> <u>categories</u>
attempt to put vocabulary into situational contexts.
Functions such as "requesting information," "hiding
your intentions," or "defending your principles" are
fairly content-free but can help enliven otherwise
inert topic lists. The topic "restaurant" elicits
both food vocabulary and ways to request information
and express various degrees of satisfaction. These
words are more likely to appear in made-up texts,
dialogues, narratives, descriptions, and **simulations**. Students may fill in blanks using the cloze
procedure or indicate a likely response to a question
or comment from a limited choice. We have already
come a long way from a list of paired associates in a
flashcard presentation.

The fourth major method of organizing words in
vocabulary lessons draws on <u>systematic</u> <u>relationships</u>
among words based either on meaning: antonyms,
synonyms, hyponyms (words related by inclusion, e.g.,
cakes, pies, and ice cream are desserts); on form:
homonyms, word families, prefixes, suffixes; or on
both: cognates. These words can appear in lists for
identification or matching. They can be incorporated

into texts in the form of completion exercises, with items like "Water is <u>wet</u> but sand is _____," or they can form designs that take advantage of the computer screen's capabilities to make dynamic word patterns.

The most satisfactory way of presenting words for vocabulary instruction may well be the use of <u>real</u> <u>text</u>, highlighting the words of interest. This is actually a type of reading lesson. Students may be asked to identify the part of speech of a high-lighted word, or to locate a synonym of a highlighted word somewhere else in the text, or to decide which word (or part of a word) should fill in a blank. Again, when the limits of simple drill are reached, we must find imaginative ways of using the computer's ability to present information dynamically.


## PRESENTATION OF WORDS


Words are presented on the screen in order to supply a limited corpus for use in subsequent exercises and, frequently, to help establish meanings. Sometimes they appear individually or in pairs, a single **frame** at a time. An easy way of presenting words is to show the relevant vocabulary file. Word groups should not, however, include more than eight to twelve words at a time.

Presentation for meaning can take advantage of the dynamic qualities of the screen. A word and its associated picture, for example, or its synonym, homonym, translation, or prefix can be highlighted at the same time. Words can be made to move across the screen to fill in appropriate blanks in sentences or to be paired with other relevant words or pictures. Words or images can dissolve and re-appear, or be replaced by an antonym or a word from the same paradigm. In the same way, a prefix can fade and be replaced by another. A word family, for example, instead of appearing in a vertical list, may be shown as a succession of transformations of a given word: "friend" becomes "friendly," and then changes to "unfriendly," and so on. To focus on meanings as

30                    II.  EXPLORING THE LANDSCAPE

well as form, illustrative sentences can accompany each new word.

Here one must seriously consider whether the printed display of native language equivalents is useful, or whether other media should be integrated into the drill, so that students can experience items visually.  Additional equipment, such as videotape and **videodisc** players, involves additional expense; these possibilities are discussed in more detail in the section on speaking and listening.  A possible compromise is the use of computer graphics to draw images on the computer screen.  Simple, cartoon-like visuals, with accompanying sentences, can supply a dynamic context for vocabulary presentation.  The image of a waiter can be displayed next to the text of a sentence in which the day's <u>hors</u> d'<u>oeuvres</u> are listed one at a time.  (Visuals can help indicate meanings here, but they can be ambiguous:  one man's meat is another man's eggplant.)  Similarly, a person can appear to give a description of a trip in the country, a visit to an apartment, or a stroll downtown, with relevant text appearing as the images are presented.

A whole dialogue can be presented in this relatively unstatic, lively way.  More elaborate visuals can be made to move and accompany sentences that describe an event or they can prompt students to describe the event.  Unfortunately, most graphics images on small computers may be little better than stick figures or coloring book pictures and thus lack the critical cultural component of a video or slide image.  Moreover, computer graphics as commonly practiced may require the better part of a minute to draw an image, or may use up large chunks of storage, so that this solution may not be appropriate for many types of fast-paced vocabulary study.  Even the simplest images may be quite time consuming to construct without special devices such as **graphics tablets**, which use a kind of tracing operation to transfer computer images to the machine's memory.  Animation is an additional level of complexity that requires special software.

# PRACTICE WITH WORDS

The computer can support countless types of
exercise to drill and test vocabulary, including
matching procedures, identifications, multiple-choice
formats, fill-in-the-blanks, and short answers.  On
the computer, the choice of exercise format involves
an awareness of the answer-processing features
available within the program.  The first three types
require a simple yes/no decision and as such demand
very little of the program.  In the case of the last
two, where the user writes a word or words, yes/no
processing may not be acceptable.  Some sort of more
elaborate analysis may be preferable.

Another general concern is the number of tries
the computer gives the student and whether or not it
automatically shows the correct answer at some point.
While a sentence structure exercise can take a while
to work through, a simple vocabulary item should not
require too many tries, particularly where guessing
from a list is possible:  two tries are probably
enough.  It is wise, however, to let the student
decide when to move on.  A simple **help command** can
allow the student to see the right answer, type it,
and move on to the next item.

The computer's ability to time events and
display animated images is often used to create
learning **games**.  There need be no radical
difference between a more serious instructional
strategy and a game.  By adding more interesting
rewards and punishments for right and wrong answers,
we can make pedagogically sound strategies and
materials take on a certain fascination that
encourages learning.  The best games do not simply
tack on cute tricks to the interaction, but use
motivation that is intrinsic to the subject matter.
Game programming, it should be noted, usually demands
the maximum of both the programmer and the machine;
it is seldom appropriate for an initial project.

It is easy to criticize game-like exercises:
they often depend on a particular motor skill without
which the most elaborate and subtle awareness of word
relationships is of no avail, and they use words as

mere tokens in a secondary, noncommunicative function.  Some matching games are fun to play, however,
and if the word list can be properly controlled by
the instructor to include productive and relevant
vocabulary that is used again in other contexts, if
rewards are integrally related to the subject matter,
and if missed items are recirculated, games can
probably play a significant motivational and instructional role.

Games of this type can be contrasted with the
ubiquitous "hangman."  Too often, the lugubrious
sequence of events in hangman depends on nothing more
than guesswork.  It is difficult to see how much real
language students actually manipulate by guessing
letters and watching an isolated phrase take shape.
Hangman-type programs appear to be of limited value,
if any; as examples of the state of the art in
foreign language computing, they are often an
embarrassment.  They also suffer from a classic flaw:
it is more interesting to make a mistake than to answer correctly.


## PERSPECTIVE


The most important lesson to be learned from
this tour of a representative landscape is that
teachers' knowledge and experience will be far more
valuable in creating and evaluating instructional
computer programs than anything they can ever learn
about computers.  Many programs will not meet
instructional goals, or will seem trivial or even
detrimental to learning.  It should be noted that
good programs will only emerge from serious reflec-
tion on methods and course content.  Good design
reflects good teaching concepts; programming must
rise to these standards.

# III

# Skill Applications

## GRAMMAR

The objectives of foreign language teaching usually stress instruction in the four skills--listening, speaking, reading, and writing. It is understood that these skills rest on a foundation of language knowledge that includes sounds, vocabulary, culture, and grammar. All language skills can benefit from computer technology to some extent. However, despite the many options and possibilities that computers and **programming languages** provide, **computer-assisted instruction** has been most successful in the teaching and practice of grammatical structures:

> It is often when applied to the grammar
> learning situation that the analytical and
> interactive capabilities [of the computer]
> have been used to good advantage. There
> are no grammatical constructions that do
> not lend themselves readily to effective
> treatment by the computer via multiple
> choice, or constructed formats. (Holmes
> and Kidd 1982, p. 508)

Even the most experienced and patient teachers become frustrated at times because much of their available classroom time has to be spent drilling grammar points, a task that takes away valuable time from communicative activities. Computerized instruction offers a solution to this problem, relieving teachers of certain necessary but mechanical efforts and providing more time to work on other aspects of second language teaching, particularly conversation. We should view the technology in terms of increasing the effectiveness of our teaching efforts, rather than as a means of dispensing with them.

Most computer programs in foreign languages deal with grammar and vocabulary. We have found that the quality of these programs varies greatly. Even some of the newer ones merely reproduce textbook or workbook exercises and give only "correct" or "incorrect" as guidance to the student.

Example:

```
COMPUTER:  verb:  venir
           1)  Julie ...... avec nous.
STUDENT:            vient
COMPUTER:  BIEN!  Julie vient avec nous.

           2)  Nous ...... aussi.
STUDENT:            vienons
COMPUTER:  NON!  Your answer should have been
           "venons."
                Nous venons aussi.
           etc.
```

Some programs will allow a second try after one incorrect response before showing the right answer. This kind of **answer processing** is unlikely to motivate or stimulate students particularly and may even lead to boredom. As a novelty, a simple process may work for a while, particularly with younger students, but we can and should expect a good deal more from the instructional computer. When students are merely told that their answer is right or wrong, their effort amounts to little more than guessing. Of course, **record-keeping** and **branching** possibilities can be built into programs of this type, making them more interesting.

CAI programs for teaching grammar range from simple **drill and practice** to elaborate **tutorials.** As the example above indicates, one type is a drill where students supply a given form such as a verb or adjective. Another simple possibility is the multiple-choice exercise where students choose the correct form. Although some teachers do not like multiple choice, these exercises can be enriched on the computer if precise and helpful comments are provided for each choice. If students are immediately told why a or b or c was incorrect, they may be less likely to make the same mistake again. Since the choices in such an exercise are limited, explanations can be clear and to the point.

Almost any simple drill can be improved if the grammar principle that is being practiced requires not only a mechanical answer but one that has meaning as well. A verb-ending drill, for example, will be radically improved if students must select not only the correct ending, but also the correct verb from a list. Teachers agree that we need more meaningful practice activities, yet CAI programs--like textbooks, workbooks, and worksheets--continue to emphasize mechanical manipulation of language forms. An interesting study by Schaeffer (1981) used a short CAI program to test students' knowledge after they had worked with mechanical and semantic exercises. Students who worked with semantic exercises performed better on both the structural test and the semantic test than those students who had practiced with structural exercises alone.

Many teachers favor tutorial CAI programs over simple drill exercises. Here, students are taught a specific grammatical concept and then drilled on its applications. The tutoring takes place on a one-to-one basis, and all instruction is geared to students' individual responses. The computer's ability to store a large quantity of information related to the student's most common mistakes provides the opportunity for tutorial advice that should help to overcome errors and reinforce grammatical patterns and structures. The advice and hints given should correspond to what an experienced teacher might say if enough time were available in the classroom. Tutorial programs have been especially useful in remedial and review work, where systems for tracking and **diagnosis** surpass what most teachers can regularly undertake.

III.  SKILL APPLICATIONS

The following example is a shortened version of
a lesson from the German program TUCO (Tutorial Computer) developed and used at the Ohio State University.

## IMPERATIVE

German has three imperative (command) forms:
The command forms of the verb <u>kommen</u>
(to come) are regular:

| | |
|---|---|
| The polite form | -Kommen Sie! |
| The familiar singular form | -Komm(e)! |
| The familiar plural form | -Kommt! |

Take notice of the verb-first position and
remember that it is the relationship between
people that determines the use of the polite
or the familiar form.

The command forms of the verb <u>sein</u>
(to be) are irregular:

Be quiet!
Seien Sie ruhig, Herr Braun!
Sei ruhig, Fritz!
Seid ruhig, Kinder!

Now let's see if you can use the correct and
suitable form of the imperative.

COMPUTER:  Herr Klein, _____ die Rechnung!
                 (bezahlen)

STUDENT:             bezahlen
COMPUTER:  You forgot an important part of
the polite imperative.  Try again
and remember to include the missing
part.

In most cases, the student would now type in the
correct answer:

III.  SKILL APPLICATIONS                 37

```
STUDENT:                    bezahlen Sie
COMPUTER:   Sehr gut!
```

Another student might have made a different mistake:

```
STUDENT:                    bezahlt Sie
COMPUTER:   Not quite.  You always need the
            infinitive of the verb to make the
            polite imperative.
            Try again.
```

Again, most students would now type in the correct answer.  However, a third student may have made yet another mistake:

```
STUDENT:                    bezahlt
COMPUTER:   This is a correct form of the
            imperative.  But which one
            should you use here?

            a.  the polite, or
            b.  the familiar singular, or
            c.  the familiar plural?

            Please try again.
```

In this example a total of eight wrong answers were anticipated; each receives an appropriate explanation.  The eight error types anticipated for this item are:

1. wrong type of imperative;
2. the pronoun _Sie_ was omitted;
3. the pronoun _Sie_ was not capitalized;
4. student did not use the verb first;
5. student used a pronoun other than _Sie_;
6. wrong verb ending;
7. student had the wrong verb ending and left out _Sie_--two mistakes were made and addressed;
8. student did not use the verb first and had the wrong pronoun--two mistakes were made and addressed.

Each of the diagnostic messages in this list is activated by a procedure known as **partial answer processing**, which amounts to examining the student's answer to see if it contains predictable wrong segments. Each **anticipated wrong answer** is keyed to a presumably helpful message describing the nature of the error. Although mistakes 7 and 8 are hardly ever made, looking for them does serve a function for the extremely weak student. Since typing and spelling errors cannot be included among the anticipated wrong answers, these types of mistakes receive a response like "Something is wrong here. Check your typing or spelling."

It takes a good deal of time and effort to write such a program. Nevertheless, TUCO includes over fifty grammar topics ranging from simple verb endings of regular verbs to the subjunctive. Once written, a program can be used by hundreds of students semester after semester, without further involvement of the author. As more sophisticated techniques of programming are applied to tasks like this, automated means of diagnosing errors are replacing the laborious anticipation of specific answers to specific questions.

Not all tutorial programs need to be comprehensive. In fact, given the time, money, and effort necessary to write them, it may be wisest to develop **modules** that concentrate only on difficult structures. This is particularly true if the CAI program is used mainly as a supplement to regular classroom instruction.

Examples cited so far use a fill-in-the-blank format. Fill-in exercises are especially useful for work with conjugations, declensions, and cases. Many grammar programs on the computer use this format because it reduces the possibilities for error. When the CAI author must anticipate wrong answers, it is much easier to handle one-word answers than full sentences.

Full sentence answers are, of course, possible on the computer. Transformations, completions, short translations, and scrambled sentences focus the student's attention on several syntactic and morphological points at the same time. Many long

III. SKILL APPLICATIONS                                    39

answers, particularly translations, may have more
than one correct answer, however. Programs that
store a number of possible correct answers for a
given item and compare them with the student's
response can be rather complex. The more words there
are, of course, the more possible errors there are to
anticipate.

Some precision in error analysis can be obtained
without anticipating errors. DASHER, an **answer
processor** for language study developed at the
University of Iowa, does not analyze answers according to grammar rules and does not use a list of
explicit verbal messages to guide students to correct
answers. Using dashes or other symbols, it relies on
precise visual strategies to indicate the location of
errors. Wrong characters in a student's answer are
replaced by dashes, and the answer is then flashed
back to the student for correction; this approach is
known as **pattern markup**. The student simply
replaces dashes with correct letters:

```
COMPUTER:   Je me lave.   (Tu)
STUDENT:    Tu te lave.
COMPUTER:   (Non.)
            Tu te lave-.
                  -->
STUDENT:              s
COMPUTER:   (Oui.)
            Tu te laves.
```

Additional symbols and messages diagnose extra letters, transposed words, and extraneous words. In
this system, multiple correct answers are still
difficult to handle from a programming standpoint.
Fully communicative items exceed the capacity of the
program. On the other hand, with this **authoring
system**, the author need only write questions with
answers to create a grammar exercise, without
anticipating possible errors and their explanations
or engaging in any programming. A graphic, rather
than verbal, diagnosis also avoids the use of English
and the use of grammatical terminology that may only
baffle students.

Good **answer processing**, not the kind that simply says "right" or "wrong," is the key to effective
grammar exercises on the computer. Whether the
system involves some sort of visual pinpointing of
errors, as in DASHER, or uses verbal explanations for
anticipated errors, as in TUCO, or some combination
of the two, good error analysis can help students
learn as they move from one item to the next. Exercises should be generally uniform, so that the
students can improve their performance as they move
from item to item. This potential is what distinguishes computer-based drill from other kinds of
written work. It is not always easy to write grammar
exercises that directly rely on and help develop real
communication. If some items must remain dumb and
inert, however, at least the diagnosis of errors
should evoke a sense of lively and meaningful
interaction.

CAI grammar programs can be made to generate
items instead of using a finite set of prefabricated
sentences. **Generative exercises** can be useful in
helping students create their own sentences. By
picking a word at random from a **pool** of possible
subjects consisting of subject pronouns, names,
professions, etc., and then picking a verb from a
verb pool and a direct object from an object pool, a
program can **concatenate** the words to form a
sentence. With regular verbs, the program will
attach the appropriate ending to the verb, depending
on the subject it has chosen. When appropriate, the
program can also add specific articles or other noun
markers, adjectives, and so forth. The pools of
items, of course, must be constructed in a way that
guarantees reasonable sentences. A program that
constructs a sentence like "The baker kisses the soft
house" may seem amusing, but it may also confuse
students. Systems can be devised that capitalize on
this possibility by asking students to determine
whether a randomly generated sentence is absurd,
illogical, or probable.

An exercise format that puts this programming
possibility to use shows students the words from the
pools and allows them to make their own sentences
following a sentence model. A simple English example

III.  SKILL APPLICATIONS                                41

illustrates this technique:

The table is green.

| | |
|---|---|
| chalk | interesting |
| window | red |
| book | boring |
| pens | smart |
| pencil | open |
| teacher | white |

Use these words to invent sentences
like the model given above.
-->

The program then searches through its own possibilities for a match with the student's attempt.  A
partial match could lead into some sort of answer
processing, as discussed above.  Sentences generated
in this way are likely to be simple and may not have
much more inherent meaning than the sentences in
traditional programs.  The process does, however,
encourage students to create their own sentences;
this limited exercise of freedom can be considered a
step toward competence.

Meaning can enter practice of this type if
students write sentences following a given pattern to
describe a person or a thing.  In sentences like the
following, the student would, in many languages, have
to indicate that "Jane" was female so that the
program could make the correct agreement with the
adjective:

Jane is intelligent.
Jane is industrious.
etc.

The program itself supplies the verb, accepts the
name the student types in, and searches a large
**file** of adjectives.  Instead of making the verb
agree with the subject, this time the program makes
sure the adjective agrees with it.  The corrected
sentences are stored and presented at the end of the
exercise as a description of the student's friend.

The text will be monotonous, no doubt, but it will be correct and--within limits--personal. In a slightly more ambitious version, the student is required to supply two names, one of each sex. Further elaboration leads the program to accept appropriate pronoun transformations for the subjects. If antonyms are marked in the file, a program can even question conflicting descriptions:

> STUDENT: Jane is lazy.
> COMPUTER: No, Jane is not lazy
> because you say she is industrious.

At this level of expressive freedom, the programming already becomes quite complex, while the sentences remain remarkably simple. This discrepancy may explain why generative exercises are not widely available at this time.

## WRITING

Most students begin writing a foreign language by doing exercises to develop form, structure, and vocabulary. These mechanics of writing respond well to computerized lessons because answers can be processed in some detail and compared to a single correct form, as described earlier. Beyond that, when writing involves free expression, particularly beyond the sentence level, there is very little the computer can do to correct errors. There are still a number of uses for the computer as an aid in the teaching of writing, however. As soon as the computer can no longer take part in error correction, the teacher simply takes over that function. As long as forms are processed for correction, exercises remain primarily grammatical. Students can become inhibited in their writing if their major concern is forming correct sentences rather than expressing themselves. The most important activity in learning how to write well is writing itself. Having errors corrected is probably not nearly as crucial as having and keeping the motivation to write. With well-planned, imaginative uses of a **text editor,** computers allow and can even encourage the production of a significant amount of writing, both guided and free.

Sentences the student types line by line, transforming a model, can later be assembled by the program into a paragraph and presented either on the screen or on paper. If the transformations are simple and involve single correct responses, the correct version can be shown next to the student's version. Students can then make their own corrections. Letting the students perform the task of answer processing themselves can be an important step in developing the skill of copyreading. At least we know that an intelligence higher than the computer's is guiding the work.

By writing out responses to a series of prompts, suggestions, directions, or queries, students can be guided to construct whole paragraphs on any number of topics. Without depending on answer processing, the range of questions is infinite. This type of exercise could just as easily be done on paper by the students. The computer, however, produces a neat, uniform text from every student for the teacher to grade, mark, or just read. Students can easily enter the teacher's corrections into their texts to improve their writing. Some teachers prefer not to make explicit corrections but to respond to student writing with questions whose aim is to encourage the students to develop their own text further: "Is that the way you always spend your summers?" "Tell me where Lake Okoboji is." "Who are Tom and Lisa?" "When did this happen?" With student paragraphs on the computer, the teacher should be able to enter comments quickly and easily, helping all students expand and clarify their own writing and thinking. Useful programs to manage these activities can be expected in the near future.

What students produce need not remain on the screen, of course. When a printer is available, the teacher can read typed texts of high quality. Neat pages with an attractive format may add to students' pride in their work. Copy produced in this way should make it easier for students to read each other's writing. Students should find their peers' texts easy and interesting to read since the structure and topic of each paragraph could be identical to texts they have produced themselves. Dialogues between teacher and writers can be supplemented by dialogues among writers. By concentrating on what people write rather than on how they write, the class can begin to explore real communicative functions in writing.

Besides responding in writing to direct prompting, students can also be asked to write using a more complex stimulus. The computer can present a telegram, love letter, or other message to be answered. It can display visual material--static or moving--on a part of the screen. These may be simple pictures or the more elaborate representions of data characteristic of some **simulations**. One typical simulation represents events associated with French trappers in the North Woods. Players choose the furs to collect and the trading fort where they want to sell them. Each variable is associated with risk and profit potential: one fort is hard to reach and the player may lose everything to a raging river, but furs bring more money there. A multiple-choice format allows students to make decisions; chance plays some part in the outcome.

As students follow the course of the simulation, they can be asked to write out in French the short narrative that the simulation develops. At each stage of the process, they answer questions to indicate what is happening. The students' writing will not influence the events; it simply recounts them.

With other simulations, students can analyze data from a graph or discuss the situation of their leaking boat, weighing the decisions necessary to save it. In this way, some of the interesting features of the computer are used to supply basic information that the student develops further in writing. The business letter, for example, can become more meaningful if it is written to account for events that are being simulated in a dynamic model of profit and loss.

III. SKILL APPLICATIONS 45

Beyond the sentence level, when students are writing texts that are not closely related to specific cues, it may be easier to have them compose on paper and transfer their compositions, by means of a text editor, to the computer. Text editors are powerful tools and very easy to use, but they may not always lend themselves to free composition. One advantage of using them for teaching composition is that students can be encouraged to compose a "final" version. From this they can print good, correctable copy that can be easily distributed, altered, and expanded, as discussed above.

## READING

"Page-turner" is a common term of scorn applied to unimaginative instructional computer programs. The transition from noisy teletypes to elegantly drawn screen images has justifiably called attention to the fact that we must do more than transfer books to video screens. Indeed, there is no good reason to transfer foreign language reading materials to computer files for eventual display to a student who is required merely to press the **RETURN key** to see the next paragraph.

The limitations of handling natural language responses, combined with a growing understanding of the interactive nature of the reading process, have led to renewed consideration of the use of computers in teaching reading in a foreign language. It may be surprising to realize that highly interactive reading programs and dynamic writing programs go hand in hand; in some cases they may be identical. The act of reading one's own writing and the act of commenting on one's reading merge into a single larger skill that the computer can help direct and refine.

Commercial "reading" programs now coming on the market treat various English language arts skills at the grade-school level. A look at any of these programs quickly reminds one that foreign language teachers are not usually teaching "reading" at all;

III.  SKILL APPLICATIONS

we are attempting to mobilize a more or less well developed native language skill on behalf of the target language. Our students have mastered a large number of text-confrontation skills that they often ignore as they are inundated with sentence patterns, endings, and isolated vocabulary.

The computer offers the opportunity to control the interaction between the student and the text and to intensify the reading experience. Texts and exercises can be adjusted to match or appropriately challenge the student's ability level. An authentic text that uses large numbers of relative pronouns can be introduced first for comprehension in a simpler form without relative pronouns. When it is clear that the student grasps the modified version, the more difficult authentic text can be displayed for further work, or the two texts can be displayed in parallel windows on the screen.

Language teachers often feel disgruntled by their students' tendency to equate reading with word-for-word translation. All too often we hear students remarking to each other that they have to "translate twelve pages for tomorrow." At the computer, access to ponies and glossaries that hinder overall comprehension of a passage can be limited. Short sight-reading exercises displayed on the computer screen can be designed to encourage both guided and spontaneous guessing about content, activating this skill systematically for transfer to easy-chair reading. Comprehension practice can be conducted under conditions that also restrict access to the text, forcing the reader to internalize the content, rather than trying to match printed questions with printed text.

The use of the computer to activate the strategies used by mature readers appears to be a fertile ground for immediate development. Text manipulation, reconstruction, amplification, modification, skimming, scanning, outlining--these techniques for discovering a text's unique structure and meaning can all be handled much more easily on today's computers than can student production of language. The possibility of offering dynamic texts--practically adventure games--means that the

III.  SKILL APPLICATIONS

act of reading should no longer be viewed as a passive skill.  Alternate styles, logical contradictions, characters similar to the students themselves, randomly selected details of landscape, scrambled sequences of events--virtually every element of a text can be manipulated in productive ways.

Many language teachers trained in literary analysis will also feel quite comfortable attempting to convert familiar strategies to the individualized environment of CAI.  For example, the narrative point of view of a Grimm's fairy tale can be made to change at the student's command.  Verb forms and pronouns, as well as more subtle distinctions in perspective and tone, would signal the changed viewpoint.  Comparison of different versions of a text is only one example of many possible strategies that can lead to a highly intensive reading experience where students are given immediate, paragraph-by-paragraph diagnosis of their level of comprehension.  The result may well be a far more interactive and dynamic approach to teaching reading than now prevails in many classrooms.

## SPEAKING AND LISTENING

Speaking and listening are person-to-person skills that obviously cannot even remotely be replicated on a bare-bones computer that communicates via a keyboard and a screen.  Even using the most sophisticated additional or **peripheral** equipment, today's computers can hardly produce the science-fiction effects needed to simulate human conversation.  Teachers, native speakers, and study abroad programs are not on the verge of obsolescence. Nevertheless, by using additional technologies, we can find fascinating ways to give students much more realistic exposure to the target language.  The limitations of the audio language lab are gradually being overcome as the computer makes listening and viewing more interactive.  The attraction of using these additional media lies in their potential to overcome the somewhat sterile feeling of computerized drill and to confront the student with authentic samples of language and culture. The kinds of technology described here, however, are expensive; many of them cost far more than the basic computer that may control them.

Standard audio tape is limited by its sequential format. The machines available in most language laboratories are not designed for **random access**, that is, for quick transfer backward or forward to a designated segment. Newer equipment can react to student performance through control of the audio portion of a lesson. This means that listening comprehension and drill materials can be given a flexible audio component. If a student has difficulty with a given text segment, the computer can immediately replay that segment. The advantages of this sort of control are manifest.

The most effective way to provide a non-sequential audio component is to use a **random-access audio recorder**. Disk-based machines are available that allow the kind of control described above at a cost comparable to that of a microcomputer. If the desired transfer between audio segments takes place fairly infrequently, or if the segments are relatively short, the use of tape players with digital playback control is also a viable alternative. Both types of equipment are controlled by a microcomputer that presents lesson text on a video screen and transmits playback instructions to the audio device.

The technology described above relies on recorded speech. A more advanced technology now reaching the educational market involves computer-generated speech, which can take two forms: **digitized speech** and **synthetic speech**. Digitized speech stores a numeric encoding of a real utterance and regenerates the utterance at playback time. Memory limitations usually require the sacrifice of a good deal of data about the sound of the original utterance, but the quality of the reproduction may still be quite good. Synthetic speech, which is only beginning to offer acceptable quality on microcomputers, involves rule-based speech production using

III.  SKILL APPLICATIONS                                    49

highly advanced microprocessor circuitry.

It is still too early to tell whether the quality of speech generated by speech synthesizers will be acceptable to language teachers. The advantage of this technology lies in its potential to create unlimited numbers of utterances, rather than having to draw on prerecorded segments of speech. The greatest drawback now is the lack of good sentence intonation. This is an area where open-minded experimentation is called for, since sound can greatly enliven current silent forms of CAI. Synthetic speech can already have an impact in native language tutorial programs using English, since instructors will be less concerned about a mechanical quality in the speech. Using synthetic speech in this manner offers a nonvisual source of information that can be used to direct the student's attention to selected aspects of text or images on the screen.

The most promising area for improving the listening skill is computer-controlled video. The advantages described above for audio are dramatically increased by the use of video. Random access video, via the **videodisc**, and computer-controlled videotape can offer the student a realistic visual artifact that may well have inexhaustible potential for imparting knowledge of language and culture. One fascinating large-scale experiment involving the use of instructional technology in foreign language teaching is the "Montevidisco" project at Brigham Young University. The project exploits all the best aspects of videodisc technology to create a per-sonalized, ever-varying video tour of a Spanish-speaking city. The students' desires and responses determine the sequence of events. Computer-controlled audio allows students to record their side of simulated conversations. Similar projects are underway for German and French.

The capacity to control a chunk of foreign "reality" cannot be overestimated as a learning tool. The disadvantages of this technology lie in its high cost and the difficulty of obtaining high-quality, up-to-date video materials.

The speaking skill is probably the stepchild of computer-assisted instruction in foreign languages.

Recording devices under computer control are available, but not widely used because students are notoriously bad at recognizing their own errors when they are asked to compare their speech with a prerecorded model. The ability of computers-- especially small computers--to "recognize" speech is still rudimentary, although machines that can distinguish among several dozen words or expressions are now on the market. Current experiments seem to show that good motivational effects can be achieved by allowing computers to respond to the student's voice. The same machines can be used as a way to insure that students pronounce words and sentences in a drill. Neither manufacturers nor teachers experimenting with speech recognition devices claim that the technology can be used to teach subtle aspects of pronunciation.

## CULTURE

The importance of culture in our classrooms has not yet been reflected in computer **software**. Though PLATO has addressed this question in a limited way, CAI programs on culture remain more the exception than the rule. A few games use cultural or geopolitical information to motivate grammar exercises; for example, explorations of Switzerland and Berlin have been linked to the correct use of adjectives or verbs.

Frequently, reading programs present cultural material in the form of straightforward facts or subtle interpretations. This may not represent much of an advance over printed media, but questions regarding customs, history, geography, and the arts can be put to the student via the computer, often through the use of simple answer formats like multiple choice and short answers. The deeper dimensions of a foreign culture, especially when contrasted with the native culture, may well elude primitive, text-oriented, discrete-choice forms of programming.

Simulations can require students to modify and interpret cultural information in any number of situations, particularly ones that involve numbers. Populations, currencies, all kinds of market events, travel factors, horoscopes, sports, statistics, geography, music, meteorology, architecture, and so forth, can be transformed into dynamic forms by use of the computer. While these presentations may be fun, they should also provide serious information that helps the student develop real knowledge.

The brightest future for computer-based study of foreign cultures lies in the use of videotape and videodisc to present authentic materials for intensive study. Some of the possibilities of these media are discussed above in the section on listening. While the focus there is on the use of recorded media for reproducing the sounds of natives speaking in a natural environment, the visual aspects of culture are obviously inaccessible to most of our students without visual media. By controlling this medium with the computer, we can develop highly structured exercises in cultural comprehension that are impossible to present in any other fashion. Computer-controlled video can go far in providing students with realistic preparation for experiences abroad, where they will have to rely on their language skills to confront the surrounding foreign reality.

# IV
# Lesson Design

## TECHNIQUES OF PRESENTATION

A few tips on the way good foreign language lessons are presented may assist teachers in designing or evaluating **software**. The transition from printed material to interactive computer material does not always come about easily for today's generation of teachers. Many good pieces of software are flawed by a lack of attention to principles of visual design and interactive **presentation**. It should go without saying that **programs** that have errors in the subject matter are unacceptable.

Computer screens often seem to be a very small display space compared to a standard 8-1/2 by 11-inch sheet of paper. Keep in mind the fact that blank space on a video display costs nothing; it is our most flexible resource in designing good displays. Many **drill** and **tutorial** programs clutter the screen with large amounts of text that the students often ignore in their desire to get on with the challenging part of a lesson. Good lessons are broken down into small **frames** that require students to make choices and apply principles. Language teaching lends itself to this approach much better than many other fields.

Pictures and color, often combined with animation, can contribute much to good lessons. These techniques should be used in a judicious and meaningful fashion to highlight relationships and aid recall. Color and drawings can actually distract the student from the subject matter.

The best programs will provide upper- and lower-case letters and foreign language characters. This topic is treated in the section on **hardware**. While foreign **character sets** are a goal we all strive for, software that does not supply them should not be immediately rejected. First of all, very few of the most successful programs in use at schools and universities or now on the market attain this standard. Second, students are usually less concerned about this problem than their teachers. Last, good programs for microcomputers can eventually be modified to display foreign languages properly. In the meantime, the convention of rendering accents with apostrophes, umlauts with colons, and so on, should not stand in the way of progress.

Well-designed programs should spring into action without extensive training of the student. These are called **turn-key** programs and systems: you turn on the machine and everything works. When students are typing answers, they should not be subjected to cryptic messages like "NON-NUMERIC INPUT" or "TYPE MISMATCH IN LINE 781" just because they pressed an unexpected key. The program should never simply stop running and leave the student high and dry. Techniques of handling this are called **"error trapping,"** and they are sometimes overlooked in the rush to market a product. On the other side of the coin, keep in mind that complex programs can never be fully student-proofed. The important criterion is whether the programs are fully **supported** by the author or manufacturer, so that problems can be remedied quickly.

Foreign language programs can be improved greatly if the number and punctuation keys are inactive when the right answer consists only of letters. Extra blanks, punctuation, and extraneous capitalization are seldom considered errors in well-designed programs. The way accent marks are typed should be easy to remember; students should not be forced to hunt and peck until they find the umlaut or the cedilla hidden somewhere on the top row of the keyboard. When programs are tested, all these features should be tried out to see whether the author has attended to detail. If not, this is a strong indication that other aspects of the program may also have been handled carelessly.

Recognizing the variability among courses and textbooks, many software authors create relatively self-contained **modules** that can be organized to suit the syllabus. Modules allow a good deal more flexibility than large, monolithic programs. Another form of useful flexibility is the capability to modify or customize the text of tutorials and drills. Language teachers are certain to disagree about terminology; textbooks are certain to make unpredictable vocabulary selections. The highest standard for good foreign language programs will allow the teacher to make editorial changes in lesson text, so that students will not be confused by conflicts or discrepancies between their computer lesson and their other materials. Admittedly, this standard introduces all sorts of problems into the design of software, but it also guarantees that programs can be altered as textbooks, courses, and faculty change. Computers offer this degree of adaptability. Teachers should demand it.

Many programs contain all the information necessary for their correct use embedded in the program. Students can obtain instructions by pressing a key or two, as directed by the program. Authoring systems and other modifiable programs require printed instructions, but programmers are notorious for their reluctance to provide full program **documentation** in comprehensible English. Good documentation is a clue to a program's overall reliability. For foreign language programs, good documentation should include a complete list of grammatical structures and vocabulary used, so that teachers can make intelligent decisions about the place of the program in the curriculum. This is especially important for programs or parts of programs that generate or select materials at random, making it impossible for the teacher to see all the forms and items by using the program.

# RECORD KEEPING

Computers count, process, and store results so well that it may be surprising to learn that many good instructional programs do not use these capabilities to score students' work. Whatever is saved or remembered ought to be saved or remembered for a reason. During a CAI session, records can be kept both on the students' performance and on their reactions to the session. Records may be used either by the instructor or by the student or both. Teachers can then check on the progress of their students through the course objectives and verify the relevance of the computer exercises to those objectives. Students can judge their own success measured against past efforts, class norms, or ideal expectations.

Records maintained on a system that does not keep track of individual students can supply information on overall questions of computer usage: How often is it used? Which exercises are used more often than others? Which items are missed most often? A general review program that is not closely linked to any particular class may help students do individual work to catch up or get ahead on their own. Records and scores may prove worthwhile here. On the other hand, the fact that Joachim gets 88.07 percent right in "Little Red Reading Hood" three times in a row, or that Olive plays "Vocab Monster" and finally wins, may not be valuable information to anyone, not even Olive or Joachim!

In general, using students' computer work to assign a grade may cause more headaches than it cures. Formal evaluation of students' performance via computer differs radically from other kinds of computer-assisted instruction; teachers should consult general references on CAI and seek the involvement of experienced professionals in designing self-contained instructional testing systems. This is an especially difficult task in our field, where simple typing mistakes can radically lower scores. Many programs that work well as supplementary drill are failures when used for testing. Students then

IV.  LESSON DESIGN

come to resent the computer--an attitude that may also gradually affect the way they treat the equipment.

The percentage of right answers is the most useful information for the program to keep track of during lesson routines. The program may include a feature that will compare this result with a predetermined minimum, say 90 percent, and produce a stock praise or regret message to the effect that the objective has, or has not yet, been met. In foreign language programs, we are constantly confronted with the problem of deciding just what constitutes a correct answer. The problem reappears here, in the area of scoring, because we do not want to provide elaborate record-keeping systems that store spurious information. As long as scores are meant only for the student's self-evaluation, this is no great problem.

Counting right answers is also a problem in language practice. Many programs require the student to reach the right answer before going on to the next item. In order to score an exercise of this type, we must work with the average number of tries it took the student to reach the answer, discounting items where the student "peeked" at the answer by using a **help command**. Even using this method, we can never be sure that we have measured knowledge, rather than typing. These difficulties suggest that multiple-choice items may be the most appropriate format when scores are considered significant.

Recorded data may also be managed within a larger framework. Sometimes the focus will be on individual students and will show their scores on a number of lessons or on one lesson over a period of time. A student's first score, last score, and best score to date on a given lesson can reveal both to the teacher and to the student a good deal about progress and difficulties. Records of this type can be displayed on a graph on which the suggested minimum is clearly marked. The program can also compute and display the mean score of the whole class, percentile ranks, standard deviation, and so on. With class records like these for a number of lessons, the instructor can effectively monitor general and individual progress.

For the purposes of program development, or **formative evaluation**, it is sometimes useful to record not only the percentage of right answers over a number of items, but also the specific items missed. The teacher can judge the difficulty of individual items and determine whether the program should be revised: if 96 percent of the users miss items 8 and 12, these items may be misleading. Item analysis of this type can also be useful in **diagnosing** areas where students are weakest, especially in programs used at the intermediate level. This type of diagnosis requires a comprehensive set of items in which each item is linked to a statement of the content objective. The program keeps track of the missed items in terms of the various objectives. Of course, if each exercise deals with a single objective, keeping track of individual items in this way is not necessary.

A very general record may be kept of the amount of time or the number of sessions a lesson has actually been used. Without keeping track of individual students, classes, or lessons, this general record can be useful in explaining or justifying the role the computer plays in the overall curriculum.

Besides relying on recorded scores and usage statistics to judge the effectiveness of the computer, instructors may insert questions following each lesson to gauge student attitudes toward item types, answer processing, and record keeping itself. The staff can determine, for instance, how students react to animated graphics, or scoring systems, or the diagnostic guidance they receive. In this way the computer can help organize its own evaluation. Our means of evaluating class instruction and printed or visual materials cannot be nearly as elaborate as the procedures we can build into a computer program. Students appreciate the chance to contribute to the maintenance and development of the curriculum through requests for their judgments. Record keeping, it should be noted, can usually be added to a functioning instructional program once the fundamental strategies of presentation and evaluation have been

IV.   LESSON DESIGN

designed, programmed, and tested.

# BRANCHING

A computer lesson is an ordered series of instructional events or **frames**. At more or less frequent intervals, many programs are designed to look at students' performance and modify the sequence of frames in one direction or another. This ability to select one sequence of frames rather than another is known as **branching**. When the program reaches the final item in a **file** of exercises, for instance, the program can either move to another set of items or allow students to make this decision themselves. The list of available choices at a given point in a program is often called a **menu**; programs that rely heavily on such selection procedures, rather than built-in decisions or open-ended commands to the computer, are known as **menu-driven** programs. For students unfamiliar with computers, the menu approach is usually thought to be the handiest method to let them make decisions, since all the information needed to select an option is presented on the screen. A single keystroke is often all that is required to make a choice.

In some **simulation** programs, students direct branching by answering questions, following different story lines through a game-like adventure. The most common kind of branching, however, occurs on the basis of the analysis of student performance. Branching goes hand in hand with record keeping and thus suffers from the same limitations: the computer must have a reliable way to evaluate performance if built-in branching is to make any sense.

Counting right answers begs a familiar but critical question: when is a right answer right? If the correct answer was "Don Quixote" and the student writes "Don Quixot," some programs will consider the answer to be just as wrong as a completely different response, e.g., "Lazarillo." Conversely, in a program where good **answer processing** guides students regularly to the correct answer, they can miss the first ten items but learn something from each so that for the next ten, they make no errors. At 50 percent correct out of twenty items, a program may well suggest an unnecessary branch. It is possible to correct for this kind of problem by having the program count a certain number of correct answers in a row and figure that into the branching decision. A program that supplies adequate information of this type to the students and allows them to follow their own paths is likely to be the most effective overall.

Branching points in CAI consist of sequencing decisions based on a systematic procedure designed to answer the question: "Is this material mastered?" A limited kind of branching may occur during the handling of a single practice item when, on the basis of a wrong answer, the program does not simply move to the next item, but presents some sort of help or analysis leading to the correct response. An example of this is given in the section on grammar. Here we will examine more significant branching decisions arising from information gathered over the course of several items or exercises.

When a program asks whether a student's performance has met a mastery criterion, three responses are possible:

1) Yes. Branch to another set of exercises either to develop the concept further (e.g., one regular verb can be conjugated, now practice different verbs of the same type), or to work on another point in sequence (e.g., the compound tense with one auxiliary is under control, now begin the same tense with the other auxiliary verb).

2) Not yet. Continue with these or similar exercises and check again later.

3) Not close. Branch back to an earlier and easier set of materials to get a fresh start.

Branching may be made to occur automatically, that is, the program need not make the student aware of the shift. Branching may also come as a suggestion to the student that since a certain level of proficiency seems to have been reached, another exercise may be more appropriate. Automatic branching is attractive because the shift to different material is not obvious to the student: there is no sense of remediation. This strategy works best in complex tutorials where the student is constantly being checked on the comprehension of new concepts and the ability to apply rules or solve problems.

In foreign language computer lessons, materials can often be organized in highly focused, self-contained **modules**. If this is the case, elaborate branching structures may serve no real purpose. Teachers and students are quite able to determine which modules are needed and select them from a menu displayed on the screen. After working on fifteen or twenty items on the passive voice, for example, students may begin to notice that errors are getting rarer and self-correction easier. Based on what they are learning from the treatment of their answers, they decide it is time for a little more challenge. They leave the current exercise and go to the following one, or check the menu to find a more appropriate module. In doing so, they are making a branching decision based on information they have gathered themselves concerning their mastery of the passive.

Exercises are often designed to follow a logical progression, so explicit branching may not be necessary for the student who simply does all the items in each exercise and always progresses naturally to the following one. It is a good idea, however, to allow students a convenient way to move ahead to more interesting and difficult questions, backward to less challenging ones, or laterally to a different but related objective. A given exercise may contain dozens of items; having to trudge through all of them may frustrate even the most dedicated of learners.

The program that provides internally controlled **selective branching** requires internal record keeping and a set of paths from one exercise to related ones. The machine is programmed to keep track of the students' scores on exercises, to compare their scores to a predetermined criterion, and to route them to relevant follow-up work. Although some CAI authors are content with a general 80 percent mastery, we suggest that the percentage be set significantly higher. Good programs allow this criterion to be set by the instructor.

Calculating only the percentage right works best for modules in which all the items are based on the same grammar point or objective. With 66 percent correct in an exercise on the partitive, the student's next direction is clear: either redo this exercise or do one very much like it until a proper level of mastery is attained. With a number of separate objectives covered in one exercise, record keeping should be more precise, or branching can be of little use.

Simply checking the percentage of right and wrong answers may be termed a content-free process. A program can also be designed to distinguish categories of wrong answers as students' responses are evaluated and to prescribe a very specific change of direction. Simple exercises where error types can be easily classified, e.g., verb tenses and gender-related forms, will lend themselves to this kind of analysis. The process should be flexible enough to identify systematic errors indicating a branching decision and to distinguish them from incidental errors.

In a lesson on verb conjugations, for instance, the student's answer can be compared to standard error patterns in which regular verb paradigms are used to conjugate irregular verbs: "vous faisez" instead of "vous faites." The program can then branch to review exercises that have been specifically designed to focus on and correct this type of error. A different error, "vous fait," would not contribute to the same branching decision. Scanning errors for specific diagnosis and treatment should lead to a tutorial step, not simply to more exercises. Writing a highly diagnostic program is a challenging task, since it is difficult to anticipate all possible errors for each item in an exercise; unless the chore is somehow systematized and

automated, is is also quite time consuming.  This
sort of analysis can be easier to program in a
multiple-choice format where some of the distractors
represent typical errors.  Showing incorrect forms to
students, however, is quite rightly discouraged by
the profession; it is no more acceptable on the computer than it would be on paper.

When students write whole-sentence answers, the
processing strategy must be more intricate.  A
student who translates "He loves me" into Miss Piggy
French ("Il aimes moi") needs work both on verb conjugations and on pronouns.  Programs can be made to
distinguish these errors and to record information
leading to the possible selection of two separate
follow-up exercises.  The program searches for the
correct form "m'" before the verb and for the correct
form of the verb itself.  The programming consists of
a sequence of several steps insuring that a response
such as "Elle m'aime moi" will not be counted right.
To make an accurate diagnosis, then, the program must
judge total correctness or incorrectness <u>and</u> focus on
the two areas of concern for possible branching:
verbs and object pronouns.

No matter how careful the design, it is hard to
be very precise in arriving at proper remedial
branching.  This is because it is impossible to find
totally reliable ways to make a computer program draw
conclusions about students' thinking, based on their
typing.  A student who has trouble with the partitive
may need work with the concept, the forms, the gender
of nouns, or with all three.  A student who uses the
indicative instead of the subjunctive may not understand when to use the subjunctive or may not know the
subjunctive forms of verbs.  While CAI authors can be
encouraged to take as many pains as possible in
interpreting errors, we can also make great progress
with simpler systems that count errors and show the
way back to easier exercises.

At a higher level of concern, branching implies
an ordered sequence of exercises designed as minimal
steps related to a rational whole.  Language lends
itself only partially to this branching framework.
Even within one grammar point there is little logical
precedence to determine that, say, mastery of the

IV.  LESSON DESIGN                                    63

masculine indefinite article should precede work with
the feminine forms.  It is, however, typically within
and between subsystems of morphology and syntax like
this that branching designs will be found.  If
students can do some exercises on the relative que
and others on qui, then the branching plan should
direct them toward some exercises where they can
practice discriminating between them and using both
correctly.  If they have trouble with these, they
should be directed back to the same or similar items.
At some point in the process, further work with dont
and the forms of lequel should probably also be put
on the agenda.

No matter how much grammar pervades our courses,
we rarely take students through whole subsystems of
the grammar at one time; dont and lequel may not be
presented until a following semester.  The computer
program that employs branching, however, will tend to
relate these forms to each other with branching suggestions so that review opportunities are not missed
and so that the notion of relative pronouns as a
systematic complex can eventually emerge and be
tested.  Relative pronouns can be made to lead into
all sorts of other areas--lexical and cultural as
well as grammatical--but there is no particular
reason to have a computer program organize many such
branches.  They can be constructed to follow a given
curriculum, of course, leading from relative pronouns
to the vocabulary of shopping to the future tense,
expressions of taste, and so on.  Branches of this
sort ought to be modifiable, so that teachers can
adjust them to the syllabus, the textbook, and the
class.

# V

# Management Tools

## TEXT EDITORS

A computer **text editor** may well be the most powerful tool placed in the hands of teachers in this century. Whether or not instructional **programs** help students, there can be no doubt that radically improved management of mountains of printed materials will leave language teachers more time to teach well.

With a text-editing program and a printer, the computer functions as a personal amanuensis who can remember and produce error-free copy. New and better products come on the market daily, but the process always involves typing and naming a document (a syllabus, a quiz, a handout), editing the text (making additions, correcting errors), indicating the desired format when printed (paragraphs, pages, indentation), saving a permanent copy, and eventually printing the text.

Parts of one text may be used to help construct another. Whole texts may also be duplicated, renamed, and then altered to construct a new text without changing the old one. No programming skills are necessary to make full use of the text editor. Because language teaching relies heavily on the printed word for daily activities, there is really no limit to the benefits this kind of system can provide.

Working with a text editor allows words, lines, and paragraphs to be corrected, moved, altered, or deleted with ease. Since the editing is done when the text is still stored as electronic impulses

rather than as characters on paper, no trace of
correction remains when the document is printed.

Entering the text involves the typing of a small
number of **commands** that are usually easy to remember: i may mean to insert a line, p to print a line,
w to write a permanent copy somewhere, s to substitute a correction for a typing error, and so
forth. Editing commands control the process of **text
entry** by which the computer acquires the document.
During text entry, additional characters are usually
typed to specify the format of the final printed copy
of the text. All these special uses of the keyboard
form the grammar and syntax of a miniature "foreign"
language that is used to communicate with the text-
editing program. Once the usage of a few keys is
learned, work with a text editor becomes second
nature.

Clever use of the storage and formatting
mechanisms of a text editor enables teachers to
create standard formats for examinations, handouts,
and other materials used from semester to semester.
The text-editing program can also create **files** that
supply information to instructional programs. A
program can "grab" lines of text from a document,
manipulate and scramble them, and print them on the
screen or on paper. As discussed in the section on
writing, students can also benefit from using text
editors in writing and revising their compositions.

Text editors handle pagination and even break
words at the end of a line, following, as far as possible, standard English procedures. The computer's
word-breaking rules tend to be fallible: they may
break "classroom" as "clas-sroom." Since foreign
words are not divided following the same conventions
as English, the **formatter** poses constant problems
of this nature and must be carefully watched. Most
text editors allow the user to turn off automatic
hyphenation.

The quality of printed copy depends on the
printer and on the type of paper used. Inexpensive
printers produce **dot matrix** characters composed of
a letter-shaped set of points. While these characters are not usually as crisp and clear as those
produced by more expensive **letter-quality** printers,

they may offer ways of generating foreign language characters. Most letter-quality printers offer foreign language type elements. It goes without saying, however, that a good deal of trial and error will be required before a computer prints perfect foreign language characters.

## ITEM BANKS

Another way of using the computer to expedite some of the paperwork of teaching is to keep files of test and exercise items on particular objectives. Over the years, most Spanish teachers have accumulated through hard work, imagination, and plunder a large and varied corpus of test items and examples for ser and estar. These have been stored in different tests, worksheets, handouts, and brochures picked up at professional meetings. An effort has been made to keep a folder with all of them handy, but sometimes the sheet with the ser and estar gems also had some clever items for saber and conocer on it and, having forgotten to duplicate it, the teacher places it in another folder. If the computer is used to store these items, they can be called up immediately to create tests and worksheets. Items that rely on visuals are generally not easy to store in this way.

There is no question that locating teaching materials and typing them into the computer is laborious and time consuming in itself. The time and energy saved come at the end of the process, not at the beginning.

An **item bank** may consist of items that are grouped according to type (example sentences, fill-in-the-blanks, transformations, personal questions, etc.). Some indication may also be included concerning the appropriate level for each item or each group of items. With careful **record keeping** and item analysis by the teacher, items can be grouped not simply according to level but also according to difficulty. Commercially available **database**

**management** programs may be the quickest route to a reliable item bank system. Home-grown programs often become unwieldy and may expose materials to the risk of being mysteriously lost.

Besides helping the teacher manipulate the file and choose items by hand, programs can choose them at random. This is particularly useful when a file has hundreds of possible items. Items must be grouped by objective and, within each objective, by item type, level, and difficulty. The instructor indicates how many items of each type are desired; the program finds the appropriate files and selects random items. With this type of program, multiple versions of a given test can be constructed. Language teachers can at last find a remedy for the painful and chronic make-up quiz. Both the file structure and the program that uses the storehouse of items can be complex. As teachers explore computers and available **software**, they should keep their eyes open for programs designed specifically to help them create test item banks.

## TESTING

Because of the very sophisticated record keeping and analysis possible on the computer, it is tempting to expand its use in testing procedures beyond the creation of the test proper. Clearly, students can take tests at the computer itself. When a test consists only of multiple-choice, true/false, or matching items, the tasks of grading and item analysis can be performed automatically and the results stored for the teacher's use. Since these item types minimize orthographic problems, they can be easily scored as right or wrong. Further analysis can generate the overall scores in a class and indicate the mean, percentile ranks, standard deviation, and the like.

At the same time, a program can analyze the responses to each item to determine its ability to discriminate satisfactorily among students. The analysis will indicate, for example, the items that were answered correctly by students who received a low score overall and vice-versa. It can show how many students chose each possible answer. These operations can also be performed on test data from paper-and-pencil tests, but each student's responses must first be entered into the computer--an investment of time that is seldom justified by the results.

By saving the teacher the labor of doing some calculations and by providing data that few teachers are willing to calculate by hand, the test taken at the computer offers a very appealing method. A number of problems suggest caution, since determining a grade is a very sensitive area. While statistics can help the teacher a good deal, some students may learn to resent the machine if it becomes associated with grading and may refuse to let it help them where it could. Even when the student need only touch one key to indicate a response, mechanical errors are possible: a key may stick, or the student may inadvertently press another key and not notice the error. Any test-taking situation can generate nervousness; on the computer, the problem may be aggravated. With whole-word or full-sentence answers, a program may test typing skills as much as it does morphology or syntax. On paper, students can review and revise their answers, correct foolish impulses, and skip items until later. Many testing programs do not allow for this degree of control, since they present the items in simple, linear fashion. Test security may also be a problem; there will always be fewer computers or terminals than students.

In lieu of testing students by computer for a formal grade, a less trying system can simply provide practice tests. Pre-tests not only help students prepare efficiently on their own time and avoid certain anxieties; they can also be used to generate the kind of data described above. Scores can help students see where they stand and can indicate when review is needed. Item analysis can help the teacher transform practice items into next year's classroom tests. It may be that once students are used to taking practice tests at the computer, they will also respond well to real tests administered there.

# PLACEMENT

Placement tests seldom cause the kinds of anxieties that graded tests do. The wealth of data that can be accumulated at the computer for use in all matters of **diagnosis** and placement suggests that these kinds of tests should be taken at the computer itself. The test will be made to distinguish any number of relevant language features, and the program that evaluates the answers will count the number of times the student makes a mistake on each of the features. A test mechanism described by Ariew (1979) for use on the PLATO system, for instance, employs some three hundred "cells," one each for a distinct language feature in French. Each item is written to focus on one or two of these cells; the program analyzes each item, looking for specific correct or incorrect forms and registering the number correct in each cell.

Results of a test of this sort should be able to reveal at a glance very precise areas of grammatical competence and deficiency. Teachers can use the results for individualized instruction and, on the basis of scores generated over a period of time, can make specific suggestions concerning the appropriate course the student should take.

# GRADING

Even if it is not possible to allow students access to computer-aided instruction, teachers may be able to make good use of a **gradebook package**. A number of such programs, designed for use in any course, are now available. They simplify paperwork (student names, attendance records, homework) and automatically perform trying end-of-semester calculations.

# VI

# Access to CAI

## HARDWARE

The two major elements of a computer system are **hardware** and **software**. Hardware refers to the physical components of the system, while software encompasses the various types of instructions necessary for a computer to perform useful work. Hardware developments in computers have been occurring at a rapid rate. **Microcomputers** are becoming more and more powerful and dropping radically in price. Innumerable books and articles are now available that can answer detailed questions about bits and bytes, RAM and ROM. Our brief discussion of hardware focuses on those topics most relevant to foreign language teaching. Users of **mainframe computers** will probably have little to say about decisions concerning hardware, unless they are contemplating a move to microcomputers. We will concentrate on microcomputers here, with the reminder that they do not all speak the same dialect--that is, they cannot always share software.

Before examining any questions of hardware, users should consider one simple piece of advice: when you find your software, you'll have found your hardware. There are great differences from discipline to discipline in the amount of **courseware** available for a given computer. The best machine at the cheapest price is useless if it cannot do something the user wants it to do. A programmer will take this risk. Teachers will progress most rapidly by sharing materials with colleagues. If a teacher is the only one in the state with a strange new machine, these benefits are lost. It is natural to be concerned about having up-to-date hardware, but one should avoid the tendency to become overly concerned about obsolescence. If a computer does its job well, there is little need to push for new models that may not yet have instructional software available.

One measure of a computer's capacity is its memory size. A typical microcomputer may have "48K" bytes of memory, that is, room for something over 48,000 characters. This space is used to store the programs, lesson text, pictures, **character sets**, and systems the computer needs to operate. Foreign language programs often require at least this much memory, either because they are complex, or because they deal with large amounts of text. Small machines can handle interesting and useful small programs and are fine for experimentation, but their ability to undertake larger programming projects is limited. For those who plan to use a **text editor**, even 64K or 128K may be too little storage capacity. The large programs characteristic of foreign language CAI also dictate the use of a **disk drive**, which enables the machine to transfer lessons and programs quickly from permanent storage on a plastic **diskette** into the computer's immediate memory. Small systems often limp along using cassette recorders, which are not acceptable for serious instructional use. A second disk drive is invaluable for development of software and may also simplify systems used for keeping records on individual students' performance.

Many microcomputers can be used with a normal television set--a relatively inexpensive way to add the dimension of color to instructional programs. The alternative type of video display is a **video monitor** designed for this purpose; monitors are essential for clear display of large amounts of text, especially if both upper- and lower-case letters are used. Inexpensive black-and-white monitors display text more crisply than many color monitors. The best way to solve problems of this nature is to try out software and hardware together before purchasing either.

VI. ACCESS TO CAI

Computers that handle foreign language character sets are clearly of great interest to language teachers. Initially, we can survive with simple conventions that replace accent marks with slashes or commas, but eventually these will be found distracting. Given some extra effort, most computers that support computer graphics can be made to display our beloved accents and umlauts without recourse to additional equipment. This practice inevitably introduces a new level of complexity into the programming, but one that adds a professional touch to a lesson.

The best approach to discovering whether foreign character sets can be displayed on a given machine may be to look at the foreign language software available for it. If someone else has solved the problem on the machine, it can obviously be done. Some systems allow users to design their own characters, placing a pattern of dots into the desired places on a grid representing the space the letter can occupy. European character sets are fairly common, while oriental characters may be impossible or require additional hardware. Language teachers should insist on both upper- and lower-case characters.

Screen displays that contain fewer than twenty-four lines of forty characters each will probably be too small; text editors require lines of eighty characters to work conveniently. Printers are discussed in Chapter V in connection with text editing.

These very brief guidelines about hardware only hint at the maze of technical questions that can affect the quality of CAI. When in doubt, teachers should trust only what they have seen working. Hardware dealers may not be able to offer as much help as experienced colleagues at neighboring institutions can, since language teachers place unique demands on computer hardware.

# PROGRAMMING

There are only two ways to acquire instructional materials for the computer: write them oneself or use someone else's. In order to program, it is necessary to learn a programming language, like **BASIC** or **LOGO**. Programming consists of constructing a valid sequence of commands to the computer, so that it will perform the intended task. Asking how long it takes to do this is a bit like asking how long it takes to learn French, or at least Esperanto: the answer depends on one's abilities and the level of skill one hopes to attain. The question for language teachers is whether there is any point in investing money and time in computers at the level of computer programming. Our answer is a qualified yes.

The qualifications arise from the fact that there is a great distance between **computer literacy**, that is, feeling comfortable with computers, and what can be called computer fluency. Many of the tasks instructors may be able to envision using a computer require a high degree of expertise. Most language teachers do not have the free time, resources, and expert assistance to acquire that expertise. A dedicated, experienced teacher-programmer, for example, could probably design and write a useful vocabulary dictation program with helpful diagnostic messages in a weekend of hard work. That amount of work would be paid off by the countless hours that students spend using the program, eliminating the need for the teacher to grade assignments or hold boring drill sessions. Reaching that level of expertise, however, could easily take months--even years--of programming practice. Teachers who find programming inherently interesting and challenging will find it worthwhile to move from simple projects to more complex ones. Others will find any contact with computers quite frustrating; for them, programming will be anathema.

While it is unlikely that large numbers of foreign language teachers will become programmers in order to meet their software needs, a minimal exposure to programming is still advisable. A few weeks' experimentation with BASIC, the programming language common to microcomputers, will prove invaluable when it comes to purchasing both hardware and software. Programming for foreign language teaching, it should be stressed, has very little to do with mathematics. Language programs that move beyond addition and subtraction are unusual. The nature of programming involves logical combinations of operations and the mastery of programming syntax. Language teachers find that these are familiar concepts transposed to a new environment.

Typical tutorials and courses in programming are heavily oriented toward numerical tasks. Language teachers hope to manipulate words and phrases, while their programming teachers want to teach how to calculate net profits. Language teachers who delve into programming will find it useful to concentrate on **string operations**, which are the techniques used to handle characters, words, endings, sentences--text. Another useful area to focus on is **text files**, which permit users to handle large amounts of sentence- or paragraph-length material conveniently.

Teachers who plan to purchase a computer should carefully scrutinize or inquire about its string-handling capabilities. If one cannot assemble groups or **strings** of characters, cannot break them into smaller segments, or cannot scan a phrase for a specific group of characters, a different machine may be needed. Much of the power of foreign language CAI derives from the ability of a computer program to store the morphological and syntactic rules of a language in the form of operations that combine or analyze groups of characters. Building an efficient verb drill in BASIC, for example, involves tacking or **concatenating** endings onto stems. To the computer the stem may bear the name "S$" and the ending the name "E$." If the computer cannot be instructed to build a verb--let's call it V$--by programming a statement like

$$LET\ V\$ = S\$ + E\$$$

users will not be able to exploit the very same

VI.   ACCESS TO CAI                                      75

logical patterns of language they are trying to
teach.  If they cannot examine a student's answer
(A$) to find the position (P) of a verb (V$) by writing

LET P = POS (A$,V$)

they will find it hard to analyze wrong answers
intelligently:  they will have trouble determining,
for example, whether the verb comes before or after
the subject in a student's response.

A brief encounter with programming will help
teachers evaluate both hardware and software and
understand their limitations.  It will also put them
in a better position to design materials that
experienced programmers can then convert into
programs.  Even if teachers do not write complex
teaching programs, they can still learn enough to
write programs that help them calculate their final
grades.

## AUTHORING SYSTEMS

Learning to program gives teachers complete
control over the capabilities of their computer.  As
programmers, they are limited only by their own
abilities and the limits of the machine itself.  On
the other hand, to accomplish a particular task, they
may have to spend weeks or months designing and
encoding their program and finding errors in its
logic, by which time the materials they have created
may no longer be needed.  One alternative to programming is to use an **authoring system** or **authoring
language**, which is a special kind of program that
has been designed to help teachers write (or
"author") lessons on the computer.

Authoring systems allow an instructor to
construct lessons at a level higher than programming:
when they construct a lesson this way, they can tell
the computer what to do using instructions that are
usually formulated in terms of showing text, asking

questions, providing right answers, and making **branching** decisions. The internal logic that handles these familiar tasks is provided--invisible to the user--by the authoring system. Well-known authoring systems are PILOT, TICCIT, TUTOR, Coursewriter III, and PLANIT. Computer manufacturers who intend to sell their machines on the educational market usually provide one general-purpose authoring system. Such systems are designed to make maximum use of the unique capabilities of the specific machine for handling graphics, sound, and student records. Many authoring systems have built-in capabilities for judging the student's answers-- including ways to ignore errors in spelling and orthography.

Using an authoring system is a fast way to enter the world of computer-aided instruction in a fairly serious but painless fashion. General-purpose authoring systems are well suited for the presentation of **tutorial** material and the use of **selective branching** to adjust the content of a lesson to student performance. Many authoring systems also have handy built-in ways of controlling auxiliary devices such as slide projectors and tape decks.

Sooner or later, the limits of authoring systems are always reached. This is their disadvantage when compared to programming. By definition, a general-purpose system cannot anticipate the most creative uses of the machine. For language teachers who desire to work with the syntax and lexicon that form the fabric of human language, the limits will be reached quite soon. The string manipulations described above are usually cumbersome or impossible in general-purpose authoring systems, although it is sometimes possible to combine the power of the authoring language with specially written routines for handling text. **Answer processing** in many authoring systems is often designed to <u>ignore</u> errors, while foreign language programs usually want to <u>catch</u> them. When the limits of the authoring language are reached, the instructor may be forced to learn programming to make any further progress.

Some of the straitjacket effects of general-purpose authoring languages are overcome by **foreign**

**language authoring systems.** A program designed explicitly for use by language teachers is, in most respects, quite restrictive but provides a way to handle a specific drill or tutorial task easily and conveniently. The instructor provides the elements of a drill in a required format; such a format is often called a **template**. Once the materials are supplied, the program takes over and handles the presentation of **frames** and the correction of student errors. This means that the instructor/author can concentrate on the design of high-quality lessons, rather than becoming bogged down in programming details. Template systems can often be expanded to meet new instructional needs, since they are usually developed and supported by a programming staff. In the foreign language field, special authoring systems are beginning to appear on the market. An authoring system is only as good as the instructional strategies built into its program. Conversely, every good program should be treated as an authoring system, that is, as a teaching mechanism that can be filled with a variety of materials to suit the changing needs of students and teachers.

## PACKAGES

The easiest way to begin using the computer in foreign language instruction is to purchase a **software package,** that is, a complete, self-contained program or set of programs sold with sufficient **documentation** to allow teachers and students to use it with little or no computer experience. Foreign language CAI packages are slowly becoming available through distributors of educational media and computer software publishers. Traditional textbook publishers have only recently begun to explore the idea of supplementing their foreign language texts with computer courseware. Packages that can be used with any textbook will play an important role in the field, especially for teachers who want to test the waters of CAI before plunging into their own projects.

In order to remain manageable and versatile, many packages focus on a single important topic, like the Spanish verb system or travel vocabulary. A few authors have attempted to cover the entire grammar of a language. Most packages deal with vocabulary and grammar, although we can expect this to change as more ambitious efforts to write games and simulations reach the market.

In contrast to authoring systems, few packages allow teachers to modify the lesson content to fit the local textbook or syllabus. This means that some determination is needed on the part of teachers who want to integrate CAI into their courses. Vocabulary selection, grammar terminology, and the sequence of grammar topics may not mesh well with a specific textbook. Students may also sense that the objectives of the package are not completely congruent with other course objectives. They may prefer to have computer materials that closely parallel their tests and homework; as a result, packages may appear not only supplemental but superfluous.

Teachers frequently express frustration not only about the quality and objectives of commercial software packages, but also about the difficulty in locating and evaluating them. Because it is rather easy to pirate computer software, and because most institutions will buy only a single copy of a package, software publishing houses are reluctant to distribute examination copies. Only improved reviewing procedures and expanded treatment of CAI at conferences can break this impasse.

Teachers may be tempted to use sophisticated copying programs to duplicate microcomputer software. Pirating programs is illegal and seriously undermines the efforts of software houses to produce high-quality materials. Teachers should request sufficient funds to support both software and hardware needs.

Most packages now available hardly justify in themselves a major investment in computer equipment. While fixed-form packages will certainly come to form an important part of a good computer library, teacher-created materials--personal work with

VI. ACCESS TO CAI                                    79

programming, with an authoring system, or with
flexible, expandable, and creative packages--will
best justify the computer as an integral part of the
curriculum.


## EVALUATION OF SOFTWARE


Evaluating foreign language software, especially
for purchase, reduces complex considerations to a
single yes/no question:  Does it do something you
want it to do in a reasonably efficient manner for an
affordable price?  It is not easy to balance the
positive and negative elements, to take the package
on its own terms while keeping one's own objectives
clearly in mind.  Until teachers have some experience
working with software, it is easy to be misled.
Published reviews with simple scoring systems are
seldom reliable, for they do not or cannot take
specific teaching objectives into account.  There is
no substitute for personal screening of a program or
package.
What follows are some guidelines that we hope
will be useful.  In compressed form, they
recapitulate points we have made throughout.
Strengths and weaknesses are intermingled; a strong
point for a simulation may be a weak point for a
drill program.  Many of the questions cannot be answered mechanically or simply, since the answers
depend on the purpose of the package and its
relationship to the individual teacher's objectives.

1.  CONTENT

What does the program or package teach?
What are its prerequisites?
What level(s) will it work on?
How does it mesh with the textbook?
  Does vocabulary fit?
  Does grammar terminology fit?
  Does grammar sequencing come close?

Are topics modular or integrated?
Is language use correct and authentic?
Does it help develop communicative skills?

2. APPROACH

Does it make sense to do this on the computer?
How much does the program interact with the
   student?
How does it handle natural language?
Does it feel lively?
Is the next step always predictable?
Is the pace fast?  Should it be?
Is it enjoyable to use?

How are drills handled?
   How does the student respond?
   What happens when trivial typing mistakes are
      made?
   What kind of guidance leads to right answers?
   Are exercise types uniform or varied?
   Are items fixed or program generated?
   Does it stress rote memorization or application
      of rules?
   Is answer processing appropriate to the
      student's level?
   What kind of help can the student get?
   Are items selected at random?
   Are missed items recycled?  Does this make
      sense?
   How many tries does the student get?
   Does the student have to type the right answer?

How are tutorials handled?
   Are explanations clear?
   Is use of native or target language
      appropriate?
   Is the student's grasp of principles checked
      frequently?
   Is branching helpful?  Is it needed?

VI.  ACCESS TO CAI

Do explanations match the textbook?  Should
    they?

Can the student be creative?
Does the computer do anything a book cannot do?
Are the materials dynamic, or always the same?
Does it simulate a cultural experience?
Does it give students access to a base of
    knowledge?
Does it let them acquire and test insights?
Are game-like elements intrinsic to the subject?

3.  DESIGN

Do students use it alone or in small groups?
Are instructions available via the program?
Can it supplement instruction?
Can it replace instruction?
Does it reduce work load?
Does it improve study skills?
Does it help students avoid errors?

How does record keeping work?
    Does it keep records from session to session?
    What kind?
    How can performance data be displayed?
    Can student comments be saved?

How does branching work?
    Is it menu-driven?
    Does it branch based on performance?
    Is branching explicit or automatic?
    Is branching linked to specific objectives?
    How is performance calculated for branching?

Can it be used for testing?  Should it be?
What is the relation between student effort and
    results?
Are typing skills essential?
Can students correct typing mistakes?
Are tone and diction appropriate?
Does it get cute and chummy too often?
    Is it rude?

Does it constantly call attention to its own
cleverness?

What about character sets?
  Is there both upper and lower case?
  Are there accents, umlauts, etc.?
  Is it convenient to use them?

Is material presented in logical frames?
Is the visual impression appealing?
Is use of visual elements effective and useful?
  Character shapes?
  Text windows?
  Text placement?
  Margins?
  Highlighting?
  Lines and boxes?
  Color?
  Drawings?
  Screen layout?
  Empty space?
  Animation?

How good is the error trapping?
How easy is it to start the program?
How much programming knowledge is needed?
Are audio elements valuable?  Can they be
  turned off?

4.  CONTROL

How much control is there over program features?
Is it possible to add or modify instructions?
Is it possible to modify items or text?
Is it possible to correct typos?
Is it possible to adjust answer processing?
Is it possible to set mastery criteria?
Is it possible to activate or deactivate scoring?
Is it possible to modify branching?
Is it possible to add whole new modules or units?

VI.  ACCESS TO CAI                                    83

5. DELIVERY

Is it compatible with present equipment?
What does it cost?
How reliable is the supplier?
What if you hate it when you see it?
Has it been reviewed anywhere?
Who has used it with students?
Is it possible to make copies?

What about documentation?
  Does the program work without any?
  Are there teacher or student handouts or
    guides?
  Is documentation readable?
  Does the documentation make objectives clear?
  Does it discuss ways to use the program?
  Does it explain how the program was tested?
  Does it list foreign language vocabulary?
  Does it detail prerequisites for each module?

How does the supplier remedy programming errors?
How can typographical mistakes be fixed?

Does the package need special equipment or
  software?
  Character chips?
  Extra memory?
  Extra disk drive?
  Color monitor for graphics?
  Monochrome monitor for text?
  Audio or video machines?
  Game paddles?
  Touch screen?
  Clock board?
  Joy stick?
  Special programming language?
  Special operating system?

Is the package available now?  Really?

6. BOTTOM LINE

Do you want what it does?
Does it do it well?
Is the price right?

VI. ACCESS TO CAI

# VII
## Directions

## EFFECTIVENESS

Although the cost of computer hardware has
decreased considerably over the years, the development of effective software and the implementation of
CAI remain both time consuming and expensive. The
usefulness of CAI programs is open to challenge. The
question, Is the time and money spent on these
programs really worth it? is a legitimate and thorny
one. Overall, the question of the effectiveness of
CAI has not been studied enough.

Probably the most celebrated study of students'
achievement when working with CAI programs was conducted by the Educational Testing Service and funded
by the National Science Foundation, which had
invested more than $14 million in the development of
PLATO and TICCIT. The study did not include foreign
language programs, however. It indicated that both
students and teachers reacted favorably to computer
teaching systems but that there was no significant
impact on student achievement: "An evaluation of two
computerized teaching systems has found that neither
has reached the potential so long claimed for this
form of instructional technology" [Jack Maggarrell,
"Computer Teaching Systems: Little Impact on
Achievement," The Chronicle of Higher Education,
vol. 17(1978), no. 9, p. 5].

Performance studies in foreign language CAI have
not been able to indicate specific trends in
achievement. Generally speaking, they have used
small samples and tested such limited areas that we

hesitate to come to any definite conclusions. In
1976, Nelson et al. concluded: "Tests of students
using CAI to learn language demonstrated that they
performed as well or better than students who used
more traditional methods, and in general the students
seemed pleased with the technique" (p. 29). Nelson
based his conclusion on studies done at Stony Brook,
Stanford, Dartmouth, and elsewhere. These
experiences with CAI programs in the late sixties and
early seventies were indeed promising, yet only a
handful of articles can be found that address the
question of effectiveness.

It is interesting to note that proceedings of
the National Educational Computing Conferences and
meetings of the Association for the Development of
Computer-Based Instructional Systems list very few
performance studies in any academic disciplines. The
most important statement to be made about such
studies is that they only evaluate the specific
software available to the target population. Since,
as we have noted, high-quality software is not widely
available, the demand for control studies seems
premature, at best. This does not mean, however,
that software developers should not attempt to
improve their products by testing them with actual
students.

While performance studies would be welcome, we
should not underestimate the time, effort, and cost
necessary to conduct such studies on a large scale,
nor should we overestimate their ultimate importance
to us. It will not be easy to control all the
relevant variables necessary to establish valid
results. Even a sound experiment is likely to focus
on only one particular type of computer-assisted
instruction, at one particular grade or level. The
Department of German at the Ohio State University
conducted pilot studies for in-house purposes and
found that good students resented having to work with
the computer on a mandatory basis, while weak
students in the control group, which did not have
CAI, complained because they were not permitted to
use it. Whether or not the computer is a required
part of the curriculum may in itself be a variable of
no small weight: students may learn best from a

VII.  DIRECTIONS

machine they can use if and when they want to.

Performance studies are hard to come by, but attitude studies are in abundant supply. Almost every article or lecture on the subject of CAI and foreign languages includes at least one reference to students' reactions to these programs. Olsen (1980, p. 345) writes:

> Almost all the departments using computer programs report some positive results. Most conspicuous is the attitude of the students. They are fascinated with computers and enthusiastic about the immediate and individualized attention their work receives. . . . Several chairpersons even attribute an increased enrollment to their successful use of computer-assisted instruction, although they do not document this claim with supporting data.

Specific attitude studies indicate satisfaction with CAI language programs. At Ohio State and at the University of Iowa, results have shown that students are satisfied with what they learn and that many of them even consider drill and practice on the computer enjoyable.

Many foreign language teachers who have developed or used CAI programs find them useful. They have described the computer in various ways: as a sophisticated tool that can most effectively enhance and upgrade instruction, as beneficial to both students and their instructor, as a great motivator, and as a teaching aid that allows teachers to devote their energies to more important work such as improving pronunciation and promoting conversation. Representative studies are cited in the bibliography.

Not everyone is pleased with CAI programs. Olsen reports numerous negative comments. She feels, however, that these remarks are usually based on "impressions, uninformed opinions, or even prejudice, while the remarks from the other group, the departments with CAI, are supported by firsthand experience and observation" (p. 342).

# RESEARCH AND DEVELOPMENT

Research and development in foreign language CAI will be driven by two forces: advances in technology and the ability of language teachers to exploit existing technology to the very fullest. The profession is just beginning to use today's computers effectively and elegantly. Even given the humblest of goals for good drill and tutorial materials at the elementary level, the available software is often disappointing.

Foreign language software for microcomputers frequently undertakes trivial tasks, or performs useful tasks badly, or reaches the market with subject-matter errors. Professional journals are only beginning to incorporate CAI into their reviewing procedures. Nationwide systems for dissemination of information are emerging, however.

As we have noted, a major concern is the lack of scientific studies of the effectiveness of foreign language CAI. Opinions diverge radically on the value of drill and the efficacy of error correction. As long as most software was either of poor quality or incapable of being transferred to other institutions, it was not tragic that so few controlled studies were undertaken. Continued neglect in this area, however, may jeopardize the ability of language faculty to obtain adequate equipment and support staff.

While we attempt to make the best use of current equipment, we must also monitor the progress of technology and research in providing the more powerful tools we need. As "small" computers gradually acquire the power of yesterday's "large" computers, the results of advanced research in artificial intelligence, speech recognition, and speech synthesis will become available for instructional use. Video and satellite technologies, merging with computer technology, will put exciting resources at our disposal. The cost of these links with foreign societies will soon be within the budget of most communities and universities. During the transition phase, imaginative language teachers should make

VII. DIRECTIONS                                          89

every effort to obtain local and national grant support for pilot programs. Teachers should be
encouraged not only to take advantage of existing
resources, but also to help create them.

VII.   DIRECTIONS

# Annotated Bibliography

The following pages contain a list of recommended further reading--a bridge from our introduction to more serious work in the field. Of necessity, the selection offered here highlights representative and useful works from a much larger body of literature on foreign language CAI. Our principle for inclusion was that a given work amplify our discussion, rather than simply repeat it. A more complete listing of published works and unpublished documents can be obtained from the ERIC Clearinghouse on Language and Linguistics. For those with direct access to the ERIC database, a search can be conducted using these descriptors: LANGUAGE INSTRUCTION (OR) SECOND LANGUAGE INSTRUCTION (OR) SECOND LANGUAGE LEARNING (AND) COMPUTER ASSISTED INSTRUCTION (OR) COMPUTERS. This search yields well over 200 journal articles and other documents.

A brief commentary/abstract accompanies each item below and attempts to convey both the substance and the flavor of the author's work. We believe that the details of previous work in CAI, reaching as far back as the 1960s, still have great value for today's developments. To make the bibliography more accessible, the list is preceded by an index pointing to articles that deal most directly with the topics we have covered here.

# INDEX TO THE BIBLIOGRAPHY

**Overviews:** Alatis, Higgins, Holmes and Kidd 1982, Lesgold and Reif, Marty, McCoy and Weible, Olsen, Putnam, Wyatt 1983a and 1984.

**Natural Language and Communication:** Barson et al., Cerri and Breuker, Clausing and Wood, Decker, Hart, Higgins, Levine, Markosian and Ager, Pusack 1983a, Sanders and Kenner, R. Sanders, Schaeffer, Weischedel et al., Winograd.

**Vocabulary:** Alessi and Trollip, Allen, Collett 1980-81, Holmes 1980, S. Otto.

**Grammar:** Adams et al., Allen, Cerri and Breuker, Collett 1982, Decker, Hope, Levine, Markosian and Ager, Schaeffer.

**Writing:** Lesgold and Reif, Lofgreen, R. Sanders, Underwood, Weischedel.

**Reading:** Collett 1980-81, Farrington, Lesgold and Reif, R. Sanders, Weible 1980, Weischedel.

**Speaking and Listening:** Adams et al., Barrutia, Curtin et al., Gale 1983a, Joy et al., Luckau, Markosian, McEwen, Mestre and Lian, Scott, Schneider and Bennion, Sherwood, Stevens, Wyatt 1983b.

**Culture:** Gale 1983a, Luckau, McCoy and Weible, S. Otto, Rubin, Schneider and Bennion.

**General Design:** Alessi and Trollip, DeBloois, Gale 1983b, Hart, Lesgold and Reif, Pusack 1983c.

**Presentation:** Alessi and Trollip, Chapelle and Jamieson, Holmes and Kidd 1981.

**Record Keeping:** Barson et al., Olmstead.

ANNOTATED BIBLIOGRAPHY

**Branching:** Barrutia, Bernhardt, Olmstead.

**Hardware:** Toong and Gupta.

**Programming:** Levine, Otto and Pusack, Tuttle, Scherr and Robinson.

**Authoring Systems:** Boyd et al., Holmes 1980, Hope, C. Jones, Pusack 1983b and 1983c, Weible 1983.

**Packages:** CEEDE, Culley and Mulford, Harrison.

**Evaluation:** Culley and Mulford, Harrison, Jones and Vaughan.

**Effectiveness:** Barrutia, Bean, Boyd et al., Curtin et al., Hope, Sanders and Kenner, Scanlan, Taylor, Van Campen, Weible 1980.

**Research and Development:** Higgins, Lesgold and Reif, McCoy and Weible, Nelson et al., F. Otto, Sanders and Kenner, Wyatt 1983a.


## BIBLIOGRAPHY

Adams, E. N., H. W. Morrison, and J. M. Reddy. 1968. Conversation with a Computer as a Technique of Language Instruction. The Modern Language Journal 52(1):3-16.

Presents the early experiments at Stony Brook. Learning tasks in the program include aural discrimination and comprehension, graphemic representation of German sounds, vocal practice, dictation exercises, written grammar exercises, English-to-German translation exercises, and vocabulary test items. Details of the general-purpose answer-processing algorithm are provided. Current work on microcomputers has yet to replicate the state of the art described in this seminal article.

Alatis, James E. 1983. The Application of Instructional Technology to Language Learning. CALICO Journal 1(1):9-12, 14.

Rejects the notion that educators, especially humanistically oriented teachers, regard new technologies as changes to be fought at every turn. Given computers' minimal capacity to deal with ambiguity, context, metaphor, or implication, humanistic teaching will play a basic role in education. In order for us to employ the new aids and equipment in a deliberate and effective way, we must remind ourselves that language learning embraces a wide range of variables and that no single method can adequately handle all circumstances.

Alessi, Stephen M. and Stanley R. Trollip. 1985 (forthcoming). Computer-Based Instruction: Methods and Development. Englewood Cliffs, NJ: Prentice Hall.

A thorough study of the uses of computers in education. Covers virtually every aspect of the field, with special attention to the design of high-quality courseware. Contains extensive bibliographic references.

Allen, John R. ELSE at Dartmouth: An Experiment in Computer-Aided Instruction in French. 1971. The French Review 44(5):902-12.

Allen's French CAI materials belong to the pioneering efforts to apply computers to foreign language teaching. One program handles vocabulary drill via translation from English to French--an approach used for its basic efficiency. Answers are edited to compensate for capitalization errors, missing punctuation or accents, and the like. Wrong answers are also checked for added letters, missing letters, and transposed errors; if there are few of these, the computer prompts the student for another try with words of encouragement. A second program provides grammar lessons via transformations that are stored verbatim and evaluated much like the vocabulary items. The third program described is a verb conjugation program that generates verb forms and analyzes wrong endings based on a stored set of rules for the verb system. Little of today's CAI on microcomputers has advanced beyond the successes of this early project.

Ariew, Robert. 1979. A Diagnostic Test for Students Entering a Computer-Assisted Learning Curriculum in French. Computers and Education 3(4):331-33.

Describes a diagnostic French test implemented on the PLATO system. Care was taken to lower student anxieties by reducing hardware manipulations, by making instructions easy to follow, by not using any timing device, and by allowing students to review answers before submitting them. Storing approximately 300 features of language, including morphology, syntax, audio discrimination and comprehension, and reading, the program assesses student competence through the second year of college French. Answer processing searches for precise features in answers of one word or more and can give partial credit when only one feature out of two being tested is missed. The program produces a complete performance profile showing areas of strength and weakness.

Ariew, Robert. 1982. A Management System for Foreign Language Tests. Computers and Education 6(1):117-20.

A computer-based system is used to generate foreign language tests. Each test is stored in a separate file; the program that assembles the test chooses one of the alternate items for each question at random, distinguishes teacher material (oral cues, answers, etc.) from student material, and formats and prints a teacher and a student version. In this way, original and make-up tests can be created from one file.

Barrutia, Richard. 1970. Two Approaches to Self-Instructional Language Study: Computerized Foreign Language Instruction. Hispania 53(3):361-71.

Reports the results of a large-scale project in which an audio program was a critical component in a machine-controlled self-instructional system. Elaborate branching strategies based on sophisticated multiple-choice items yielded very encouraging statistics when student learning was compared to that of control groups taught by both faculty and teaching assistants.

Barson, John, Robert Smith, David Levine, Maryse Scholl, and Pierre Scholl. 1981. University-Level CAI in French. In University Level Computer-Assisted Instruction at Stanford: 1968-1980, Patrick Suppes, ed. Stanford: Institute for Mathematical Studies in the Social Sciences, Stanford University.

Describes an experiment in French CAI that combined computer work with regular classwork. The program incorporated the following ideas and techniques: reliance on the rationalist direct method of instruction; division of the curriculum into strands; random-access audio; error diagnosis using a phonetic reduction algorithm for word matching. It is concluded that while the error-analysis approach was a major innovation, knowledge-based answer evaluation is essential.

Bean, Katrin T. 1978. Foreign Language Teaching at the Undergraduate Level. Modern Language Journal 62(8):420-22.

Brief report on a symposium that included talks on the Ohio State CAI project in German. The advantages of CAI for tutorial work are pointed

out, based on the use of exercises where multiple anticipated wrong answers are linked to
diagnostic messages that guide the student to
the correct answer. Students in an OSU CAI
program achieved better results than those
taught in traditional fashion. In one of the
talks summarized here, Werner Haas, the
originator of the OSU project, outlines his
prognosis for the close collaboration between
CAI work and individualized instruction.

Bernhardt, Lewis. 1975. Computer-Assisted Learning
in Russian: Some Notes on Work in Progress.
Russian Language Journal 29(103):71-84.

Details the author's work in Russian CAI, which
includes a full-course sequence of drills with
remedial branching, random selection of items
and sentence generation, vocabulary and cultural
lessons, and the beginnings of a CAI authoring
system for Russian exercises.

Boyd, Gary, Arnold Keller, and Roger Kenner. 1981.
Remedial and Second Language English Teaching
Using Computer Assisted Learning. In Computer
Assisted Learning; Selected Proceedings from the
CAL 81 Symposium, Leeds, 8-10 April 1981,
P. R. Smith, ed. New York: Pergamon Press.

Describes work in providing simple template
software for ESL and other teachers to write
lessons and in providing a measure of artificial
intelligence and auto-adaptation, via a student-
constructed sentence diagnosis and remediation
package. The article address several questions:
To what extent can access procedures and frame
formats be standardized? How much data needs to
be collected? How should programs be
documented? Evaluation data is also presented.

CEEDE (Center for Educational Experimentation, Development and Evaluation), University of Iowa. 1983. Survey Report on Identified Microcomputer Courseware for Foreign Language Instruction. Iowa City, IA.

Project report of data collected under a federally funded study of needs and development opportunities for educational computer software for foreign language instruction in schools. Lists specific software for various foreign languages, gives capsule critiques if available, and provides names and addresses of software sources.

Cerri, Stefano and Joost Breuker. 1981. A Rather Intelligent Language Teacher. Studies in Language Learning 3(1):182-92.

Introduces a system that allows authors to write CAI programs that exhibit some aspects of artificial intelligence. In an operational lesson on subordinating conjunctions in Dutch, Italian, English, and French, linguistic information is analyzed in terms of the general knowledge domain and possible associated misconceptions. Student translations of an appropriate conjunction in a sentence are classified in terms of error type and only lead to correction when a particular misconception can be diagnosed. The lesson itself seems simple and the program very complex. The problems of having a program scan for particular meanings and parse natural language errors, however, represent an important challenge to the profession.

Chapelle, Carol and Joan Jamieson. 1983. Language Lessons on the Plato IV System. System 11(1):13-20.

Outlines capabilities of the Plato IV mainframe system at the University of Illinois (Urbana-Champaign), with many examples of courseware available in reading, writing, and listening. Lessons include work not only on the individual sentence level but also with larger units of discourse. Clever uses of graphics, the touch-sensitive screen, and audio devices combine to provide many intriguing lesson possibilities.

Clausing, Gerhard and Cecil Wood. 1974. The Computer-Tutor in Media-Aided Language Programs. NALLD Journal 8(3):11-20.

Describes an early tutoring program in German grammar. A cumulative series of drills teaches, reinforces, and tests one grammatical point at a time. Answer processing flashes correct words in the correct position, leaving everything else blank. After four tries the student sees the right answer and moves to the next item. The program allows some controlled movement back and forth among exercises and has a bilingual glossary function. Each sequence of pattern drills culminates in a related reading assignment.

Collett, M. John. 1980 and 1981. Examples of Applications of Computers to Modern Language Study. System 8(3):195-204 and 9(1):35-40.

A two-part article describes the genesis and refinement of a project in which reading and vocabulary were the focus, and the response mode was strictly multiple choice. Three types of frame were initially devised: a single item of vocabulary in context; a choice of responses to mini-situations or brief conversational extracts; and questions on longer texts provided in printed form. Extension of the system to units on grammar led to additional frame types: a choice of French to English paraphrases; a choice of grammatical descriptions to define the function of a word in a sentence; a gap in a French sentence to be filled by one of the answers; selection of a letter key indicating the correct order for words in a phrase; and advanced frames that define a grammatical

function and ask students to find the correct
example. Usage printouts indicated that
students made little use of the materials until
the lessons were closely correlated with the
textbook and the syllabus. The second section
of the article demonstrates the use of computerized information retrieval to provide better access to grammatical explanations in a
textbook and to supplementary materials in other
textbooks and the language laboratory.

Collett, M. John. 1982. A Tenses Computer Program
for Students of French. Modern Language Journal
66(2):170-79.

Describes development of a program on French
verb forms. TENSES constructs sentences in a
given tense. Wrong answers elicit a simple "no"
followed by the correct answer. A help function
displays a summary of the verb forms required
for that tense. Students may ask the machine to
keep track of their best time on a drill. Most
of the discussion centers on the programming
used to construct sentences and verb forms.
Concatenating elements of a verb to form a given
tense and using that within a larger concatena-
tion of verbal elements to construct an
acceptable sentence represent an interesting
programming challenge; the problems and possibilities of such a task are outlined in some
detail.

Culley, Gerald R. and George W. Mulford, eds. 1983.
Foreign Language Teaching Programs for
Microcomputers: A Volume of Reviews. Newark,
DE: University of Delaware. ED 234 647.

Foreign language software reviews written by
high school teachers and supervisors of foreign
languages who participated in an NEH Summer
Institute. The reviews are an excellent
introduction to the evaluation of software and
the weaknesses of current materials. Sources of
software and information are listed. Few of the

reviews are raves.

Curtin, Constance, Clayton L. Dawson, Nolen Proven-
zano, and Philip Cooper. 1976. The PLATO
System: Using the Computer to Teach Russian.
Slavic and East European Journal 20(3):280-92.

Outlines developments in the PLATO Russian
project: work in learning the alphabet, both by
manipulation of words and by use of a random-
access audio recorder to play cognates displayed
on the screen; visual approaches to sentence
intonation; pronunciation; telling time; and
record keeping. Data was collected on the use
of various drill types and on student performance. PLATO and non-PLATO students showed
no significant difference in grades, although A
and B students appeared to benefit measurably.

DeBloois, Michael. 1983. Improved Approaches for
Designing Foreign Language Instruction, In
Foreign Language Instructional Technology
Conference Proceedings, 21-24 September, 1982.
Monterey, CA: Defense Language Institute. ED
236 910.

Recommends that CAI authors develop a design
model that describes how they produce materials.
People who produce language-teaching lessons
tend to base their work on invalid assumptions:
delivery is linear; audiences are homogeneous;
development is sequential; certain media
dominate; validation is too limited; resources
and lesson materials are separated; and dissemination of materials is too restricted.
Courseware authoring for videodisc requires mul-
tidimensional thinking and advanced design
tools.

Decker, Henry W. 1976. Computer-Aided Instruction in French Syntax. Modern Language Journal 60(5-6):263-67.

Interesting programs for instruction in grammar must be able to deal with syntactic problems. The technique should be powerful enough to suggest applications not duplicated in classroom exercises. One such program for handling pronominalization is described. A more ambitious program, ZAP, allows students to enter a sentence into the computer and then direct the computer to perform grammatical operations on that sentence. Routines are available for performing all desired grammatical operations on a simple sentence and a degree of embedding of one sentence within another. Three instructional stages can be integrated into computer programs dealing with grammatical problems: illustrating the operation by having the computer perform it; drill, in which both student and computer perform the operation and the results are compared; and testing, during which the success or failure of the comparison is counted. Use of the computer only as a full-fledged teacher of designated course segments is advocated over merely adjunct kinds of use.

Farrington, Brian. 1982. Computer Based Exercises for Language Learning at University Level. Computers and Education 6(1):113-16.

Describes a program that takes elementary and intermediate students through a piece of continuous foreign language text and asks questions along the way. A large set of questions, comments, and answers is used to provide informative feedback to the student.

Gale, Larrie E. 1983a. Montevidisco: An Anecdotal History of an Interactive Videodisc. CALICO Journal 1(1):42-46. ED 236 910.

Describes the project, analyzes its instructional design and purposes, discusses problems, and presents preliminary results.

Gale, Larrie E. 1983b. Using Research-Based Principles to Design Student-Controlled Interactive Videodiscs: Do the Old Rules Still Apply? In Foreign Language Instructional Technology Conference Proceedings, 21-24 September, 1982. Monterey, CA: Defense Language Institute.

A comprehensive checklist useful for all forms of interactive instruction based on research in communication, cross-cultural training, visual literacy, learning psychology, and other behavioral sciences. The checklist is accompanied by a selected, annotated bibliography of learning research.

Harrison, John S. 1983. Foreign Language Computer Software: What? Where? How Good? Northeast Conference on the Teaching of Foreign Languages Newsletter 13(1):26-30.

A software survey listing most of the available courseware and providing helpful comments on individual packages.

Hart, Robert S. 1981. Language Study and the PLATO System. Studies in Language Learning 3(1):1-24.

A thorough and explicit introduction to the PLATO IV system at the University of Illinois at Urbana-Champaign, particularly in its application to foreign language study. A discussion of the hardware, including the light-sensitive touch panel, random-access audio device, and the "intelligent" terminals (which have some processing functions of their own), is accompanied by an analysis of the instructional sequencing logic used in lesson design and instructional management. Also describes TUTOR, the interactive programming language used on PLATO IV, with the capability to support non-Roman writing systems, graphics, pattern markup for answer processing, and database management. There is a brief survey of the extensive language materials available and discussions of lesson types and problems of evaluation. This very rich network of CAI possibilities is being further developed to increase sensitivity to meaning in language, to improve the analysis of grammar errors, to make instructional strategies more flexible, and to explore the possibilities of simulations. This article introduces a special issue of Studies in Language Learning entitled the "Plato System and Language Study," which contains a number of additional articles not included here.

Higgins, John. 1983. Computer Assisted Language Learning. Language Teaching 16(2):102-14.

A state-of-the-art article with a substantial bibliography and some probing and forward-looking points of view. CAI that deals with word morphology and syntax at the single sentence level is retrogressive. The computer should not be used simply to address the conscious process of language learning through grammar drills, ostensibly freeing the classroom for more natural conversation and language acquisition. The computer can provide elements of caretaker speech. It should function more as a playmate, tool, or resource than as a teacher. The learner, rather than the program, should initiate and direct the experience. Synthetic approaches use programs that create their own text; in analytic techniques, students perform exercises on a body of text stored in the machine.

Holmes, Glyn. 1980. A Contextualized Vocabulary Learning Drill for French. Computers and the Humanities 14(2):105-11.

Describes a contextualized vocabulary program. Students use the program only after studying vocabulary lists, reading passages that contain the words, and participating in class discussion. The exercises involve completing a sentence with the correct word; the sentence is written to provide contextual clues. A help function supplies definitions of the word; two tries are given; missed items are recirculated. The blanks show the number of letters and accents required. Contextually valid but incorrect responses elicit an appropriate comment. With a near but not exact match the program will suggest a spelling error may have been made. The article includes many examples and a detailed discussion of the types of contextualization used.

Holmes, Glyn. 1983. Creating CAL Courseware: Some Possibilities. System 11(1):21-32.

Discusses three ways of producing courseware with examples of authoring systems, freeform systems, and hybrid systems, showing for each the type of exercise format it supports, the answer processing, and the feedback available to students. Template systems require no programming skills to use but are limited in answer analysis. In freeform systems, each computer-assisted learning lesson is programmed independently. A good deal of programming is needed, but dynamic screen functions and precise answer processing can be achieved. Hybrid systems are combinations of an authoring system with a freeform system. With the ease of use of one method and the flexibility of the other, the hybrid system appears to offer the best overall approach.

Holmes, Glyn and Marilyn E. Kidd. 1981. Serving
   Learner Needs: From Teletype to Micro. System
   9(2):125-32.

Recommendations based on development of CAI
programs for French, German, and Italian.
Programs are an optional supplement to
traditional learning activities. Learner con-
venience is paramount; learner control is
preferred over elaborate but compulsory branching strategies. Scoring systems are discussed.
The use of flexible screen management, cursor
control, simulated movement, and color is
advocated.

Holmes, Glyn and Marilyn E. Kidd. 1982. Second-
   Language Learning and Computers. Canadian
   Modern Language Review 38(3):503-16.

Excellent state-of-the-art article. Following
an overview of the history of CAI, the
relationship of computer functions to language
learning is discussed in terms of the presentation of data, the analysis of input, and the
interaction with the learner. Language skills
considered are grammar, vocabulary, reading
comprehension, translation, aural comprehension,
and oral proficiency. Limitations of the
computer are seen in the difficulty of handling
the subtleties and complexities of human speech,
especially spontaneous writing and speaking.

Hope, Geoffrey. 1982. Elementary French Computer-
   Assisted Instruction. Foreign Language Annals
   15(3):347-53.

Describes a comprehensive set of elementary
French grammar exercises. Using a foreign
language authoring system, exercises are both
easy to write--all that is required is the item
and its answer in a given format--and useful for
students. Answer processing replaces incorrect
letters and words with an underline so students
can see how many letters are required and make

their own corrections. A survey of users
indicated the program was popular and useful,
particularly with beginners.

Jones, Christopher. 1982. STORYBOARD. A Reading
Skills Program. London: WIDA Software.

An authoring program that allows teachers to
enter texts for exploration by students. The
text must be discovered by the student, who
guesses at possible words. English, French, and
German characters are supported.

Jones, Nancy Baker and Larry Vaughan, eds. 1983.
Evaluation of Educational Software: A Guide to
Guides. Chelmsford, MA: Northeast Regional
Exchange.

A comprehensive sourcebook on evaluation of
microcomputer software. Ten different
approaches to evaluation are documented. Review
forms are included. A resource section lists
books, directories, articles, clearinghouses and
information centers, periodicals and reports
devoted to software reviews, and computer-
accessible databases.

Joy, Barrie, Andrew Lian, and Rosalie Russell. 1983.
Listening Comprehension in Foreign Languages:
Computing Some Possibilities. Babel 18(2):15-
30.

A comprehensive approach to harnessing video and
audio technologies to the computer for optimum
learner benefits. The proposed model consists
of three phases in the use of authentic texts
for listening comprehension: global inferencing
and hypothesis making; dissection of the components of the text; and a return to the whole
text together with further listening practice.
Technologies discussed include speed-adjusted
audio, filtered audio, and videodisc.

Lesgold, Alan M. and Frederick Reif. 1983.
Computers in Education: Realizing the
Potential. Report of a Research Conference,
Pittsburgh, Pennsylvania, November 20-24, 1982.
2 vols. Washington, D. C.: U. S. Government
Printing Office (1983-381-054:134/5).

Report of a conference that explored the future
of CAI from the standpoints of learning theory,
cognition, motivation, and artificial intelligence; a key work for setting tomorrow's
priorities, especially in the areas of reading
and writing.

Levine, David R. 1981. Computer-Based Grading for
German Grammar Instruction. In University Level
Computer-Assisted Instruction at Stanford:
1968-1980, Patrick Suppes, ed. Stanford:
Institute for Mathematical Studies in the Social
Sciences, Stanford University.

Describes an approach to answer processing
capable of dealing with large, structured
responses in which the order of elements may
vary widely. Evaluation is based on built-in
grammatical knowledge and general algorithms,
augmented by a structural description of the
expected response. The analyzer performs a comprehensive check of rules and attempts to infer
mislearned rules underlying wrong responses.

Lofgreen, Charlotte D. 1983. Computers and College
Composition. CALICO Journal 1(1):47-50.

Describes a number of programs using the computer as a tool in writing essays in the native
language; the principles of design apply to
foreign language composition as well. These
programs prompt writers to choose a subject and
to develop information about it; check spelling,
punctuation, and certain grammatical or
stylistic features; and assist students in following logical steps.

Luckau, Paul. 1983. "Klavier im Haus"--An Annotated
   Version. In Foreign Language Instructional
   Technology Conference Proceedings, 21-24
   September, 1982. Monterey, CA: Defense
   Language Institute. ED 236 910.

Description of the preparation of interactive
video materials based on a short television
vignette depicting life in a modern German
apartment house. Questions concentrate on
language analysis--mostly vocabulary and
expressions--and cultural exploration, as well
as the feelings, gestures, moods, and
significant movements of the people in the film.
A template system is used to create the
annotation, samples of which are included.

Markosian, Lawrence Z. 1983. A Computer-Based
   Language Instruction System. In Foreign
   Language Instructional Technology Conference
   Proceedings, 21-24 September, 1982. Monterey,
   CA: Defense Language Institute. ED 236 910.

Overview of the Stanford project to use computers as the principal medium of instruction,
especially for the uncommonly taught languages,
with serious efforts to capitalize on recent
work on artificial intelligence. The pilot
language chosen was Armenian. Eighty lessons
presenting both expository material and language
drills were developed, with additional advanced
drills. VOCAL, a curriculum author language and
lesson compiler, was used. A language drill
generator allowed the creation of materials
without requiring specification of individual
items. The project used speech synthesis technology to produce high-quality English and
Armenian speech to accompany the lessons.

Markosian, Lawrence Z. and Tryg A. Ager. 1983.
Applications of Parsing Theory to Computer-
Assisted Instruction. System 11(1):65-77.

A detailed discussion of the use of the computer
in parsing sentences, that is, in recognizing
grammatical forms and rejecting ungrammatical
ones, within a language-teaching context. The
article is technical but provides a good
introduction to a difficult problem.

Marty, Fernand. 1981 and 1982. Reflections on the
Use of Computers in Second-Language Acquisition.
System 9(2):85-98 and 10(1):1-11.

A comprehensive two-part article based on the
author's many years of experience with the PLATO
system, especially in the development of high-
quality French lessons. The following topics
are treated: factors affecting growth of
foreign language CAI; minimum standards for
acceptable programs; impact on numbers of
teachers; measuring the effectiveness of CAI;
conditions under which students will find CAI
valuable; gains students can expect; the role of
the typical language teacher in computerized
instruction; and the future of the field,
particularly with reference to computer-
controlled audio and video devices. The basic
advantage of using computerized materials
appears to be the increased degree of students'
concentration over longer periods of time.

McCoy, Ingeborg H. and David M. Weible. 1983.
Foreign Languages and the New Media: The
Videodisc and the Microcomputer. In Practical
Applications of Research in Foreign Language
Teaching, Charles J. James, ed. Lincolnwood,
IL: National Textbook Company.

A thorough overview of developments in the
field, with useful references to specific
research in learning and media usage.

McEwen, Nelly. 1977. Computer-Assisted Instruction in Second-Language Learning: An Alberta Project. <u>Canadian</u> <u>Modern</u> <u>Language</u> <u>Review</u> 33(3):333-43.

Describes a representative early project in French CAI aimed at the listening, reading, and writing skills. Data is provided on the time various learner groups required to complete computer lessons. Random-access audio, slides, and video text were integrated into grammar units that consisted of a presentation phase, a recognition phase, and a response phase. Positive student reactions are cited. A major strength of the lesson design is a flexible approach to differing student learning styles which allows students a choice of how and when grammar explanations are presented in relationship to structural practice.

Mestre, M-C. and A-P. Lian. 1984. The Use of Video in a Communicative Approach to Learning French. In <u>Videology</u>, O. Zuber-Skerritt, ed. London: Kogan Page.

Describes a range of possible uses for video in the teaching of French. Techniques examined include the viewing and analysis of authentic documents, video self-confrontation within the framework of both micro- and macro-simulations, the analysis of student performances, and computer-generated simulations. Video is an excellent tool for developing awareness of critical features of the target language and for defining the individual needs of students.

Nelson, G. E., Jean Renard Ward, Samuel H. Desch, and Roy Kaplow. 1976. Two New Strategies for Computer-Assisted Language Instruction (CALI). <u>Foreign</u> <u>Language</u> <u>Annals</u> 9(1):28-37.

By going beyond drill programs that anticipate specific answers or mark answers wrong without providing a reason, two exemplary strategies

make fuller use of the computer's power. The
first teaches German reading by allowing the
student to ask questions about a text's
individual sentences: verb forms; noun phrases;
the meaning, pronunciation, and etymology of
words; the overall translation; and, eventually,
the student's understanding. The second
strategy is based on a general model of German
word order contained in a program. The word-
order model provides a way to give helpful
diagnostic messages, which grow more and more
precise in response to students' errors. Such
general models should be combined with selective
error anticipation to overcome the rigid format
of earlier CAI exercises. Suggestions are made
concerning the most productive directions for
future work in CAI.

Olmstead, Hugh M. 1975. Two Models of Computer-
Based Drill: Teaching Russian with APL. Slavic
and East European Journal 19(1):11-29.

A detailed presentation of two Russian drill
programs and the methods used to achieve very
useful results. The first, a genitive plural
drill, is characterized by a simple
transformation of one case form to another, but
is embedded in sequencing and selection options
of some complexity. The student has a large
measure of control over the types of items
presented. Items are based on a classification
of Russian nouns. The program also controls the
level of difficulty of the items, as determined
by accumulated usage statistics. The second
program, covering active and passive voice,
takes a generative approach to creating items.
The mechanisms by which the requisite grammar
has been programmed are fully explained. The
pros and cons of generative approaches are
outlined in terms of specialization, economy,
creativity, and error diagnosis.

Olsen, Solveig. 1980. Foreign Language Departments
and Computer-Assisted Instruction: A Survey.
Modern Language Journal 64(3):341-49.

Results of a survey of institutions using
foreign language CAI conducted in 1978-79, just
before the impact of microcomputers. The status
of American CAI is reflected in a compilation of
attitudes and experiences common to many
institutions. Among the factors discussed are
cost, resistance among teachers, lack of
documented results, impact of misconceptions,
lack of trained personnel, lack of programs
suited to specific needs, and lack of adequate
facilities. The main use of CAI is to be found
in first year programs and is aimed at
vocabulary and grammar. Two appendices list
departments and programs using CAI. While the
specific data may now be outdated, the overview
of concerns continues to reflect the state of
affairs, with the exception that microcomputers
have reduced concerns based on cost.

Otto, Frank. 1983. How Teacher-Independent Can CAI
Courseware Be? In Foreign Language
Instructional Technology Conference Proceedings,
21-24 September, 1982. Monterey, CA: Defense
Language Institute. ED 236 910.

Stresses the importance of teacher involvement
in all phases of foreign language CAI from
design to implementation to evaluation. The
central purpose of CAI is to expedite certain
aspects of the teaching/learning process:
presentation, reinforcement, application, and
testing; the teacher cannot be replaced. Six
CAI research concerns for the future are
outlined: Do students learn more in less time?
Are levels of performance higher? Is retention
greater? Is teacher and student satisfaction
greater? Can innovative design principles
reduce cost? Can computers themselves reduce
implementation and maintenance costs for
software?

Otto, Sue E. K.   Videodisc Image Retrieval for
    Language Teaching.   System 11(1):47-52.

    Outlines the rationale, structure, and use of
    computer-controlled videodisc systems in the
    presentation of slides for foreign language
    instruction.   A videodisc with 54,000 still
    images can be connected to a computer that has
    been programmed both to store different kinds of
    information about each image (including the les-
    sons they support) and to access the images in a
    variety of groupings.   This configuration can be
    a flexible tool for many types of foreign
    language lessons including full-class and
    individual instruction.

Otto, Sue E. K. and James P. Pusack.   1983.   String-
    ing Us Along:   Programming for Foreign Language
    CAI.   CALICO Journal 1(2):26-33, 47.

    The general issue of programming is discussed in
    layman's terms.   An introductory programming
    course designed specifically for foreign
    language teachers provides a model for similar
    courses.   A separate section tackles more
    advanced questions related to the manipulation
    of text.

Pusack, James P.   1983a.   Answer-Processing and Error
    Correction in Foreign Language CAI.   System
    11(1):53-64.

    The way the student's response is handled is of
    central importance to the development of high-
    quality CAI in foreign languages.   Five
    categories of answer processing for drill
    programs are described:   nonevaluation,
    right/wrong evaluation, pattern markup, error
    anticipation, and parsing.   Each strategy is
    explained in terms of its operation, its
    advantages and disadvantages, its ease of use
    for authoring courseware, and its capability to
    support individualized instruction.

Pusack, James P. 1983b. <u>DASHER</u>: <u>An</u> <u>Answer</u>
<u>Processor</u> <u>for</u> <u>Language</u> <u>Study</u>. Iowa City, IA:
CONDUIT.

A foreign language authoring system that uses
pattern markup to handle the evaluation of
answers for English, French, German, Spanish,
and other languages employing the Latin
alphabet.

Pusack, James P. 1983c. A User Design Program for
Apple II. In <u>Foreign</u> <u>Language</u> <u>Instructional</u>
<u>Technology</u> <u>Conference</u> <u>Proceedings</u>, <u>21-24</u>
<u>September</u>, <u>1982</u>. Monterey, CA: Defense
Language Institute. ED 236 910.

Past efforts do not represent models of
efficient foreign language CAI, either because
it was too hard to develop the materials, or
because it is too hard to use them, or both.
Design criteria that will help avoid these
pitfalls are discussed: a proven and tested
teaching/learning strategy, flexibility in
usage, and adaptability to the curriculum.
These criteria are applied specifically to
authoring systems and self-contained packages.

Putnam, Constance E. 1983. Foreign Language
Instructional Technology: The State of the Art.
<u>CALICO</u> <u>Journal</u> 1(1):35-41.

A critical survey of recent developments in the
field, particularly as presented in recent conferences. Discusses specifics, such as games,
drill, and interactive video, and larger
questions involving the use of technology in
education, such as funding, pedagogic usefulness, and research.

Rubin, Joan. 1983. Video Design and Methodology for Foreign Language Teaching. In Foreign Language Instructional Technology Conference Proceedings, 21-24 September, 1982. Monterey, CA: Defense Language Institute. ED 236 910.

Overview of the advantages of using interactive video in language teaching: realistic interaction, simulated conversation, problem solving, nonlinear presentation, speed of access to materials, student participation, and adjustment to student differences. The constraints imposed by cost and complex development requirements are noted. Videodisc technology is an exciting supplement where knowledge about real phenomena is essential, where context is important as a clue to interpretation, and where the need for sensitive attention to expression and interpretation is critical.

Sanders, Alton F. and Ruth H. Sanders. 1983. Spion: "Intelligent" Games for German Language Teaching. In Foreign Language Instructional Technology Conference Proceedings, 21-24 September, 1982. Monterey, CA: Defense Language Institute. ED 236 910.

The program SPION combines machine understanding of natural language with the capacity to recognize grammar errors. The player communicates with SPION in two types of sentences, the command and the question, which are used to discover the correct path for getting from the airport in West Berlin to town, to find and interpret clues necessary for obtaining secret information, and to perform other spying tasks. Details on program design and instructional strategies are provided, along with a list of references on artificial intelligence related to the project.

Sanders, David and Roger Kenner. 1983. Whither CAI?
The Need for Communicative Courseware. System
11(1):33-39.

Criticizes the use of drill-oriented, stimulus-
response formats to teach grammar with the computer. Attempts are made to devise more communicative, discourse-oriented material that
uses the computer's preeminent ability as an
interactive partner. Student attitudes to those
materials are reported. One particularly
interesting discovery was the social aspect of
CAI: the way students group around a machine to
help and encourage each other.

Scanlan, Richard T. 1980. Computer-Assisted
Instruction in Latin. Foreign Language Annals
13(1):53-55.

An update on the PLATO Latin program after seven
years of use. The computer portion of the
course consists of forty lessons. The lessons
provide drill and practice in vocabulary,
morphology, and syntax; they are concluded with
a self-test. A survey revealed a substantial
improvement in efficiency of studying. A check
of the third semester class one year later
revealed better performance by about one grade
level by those students who had worked with
PLATO. Computer work counts as one-fourth the
total course grade, and students cannot pass the
course if they fail the PLATO section. Twelve
advantages of CAI are listed, including student
choice of topics and sequence; immediate reinforcement or correction; recycling of missed
items; elaborate judging of sentence responses,
with helpful comments; and the capability to
conduct diagnostic testing.

Schaeffer, Reiner H. 1981. Meaningful Practice on
the Computer: Is It Possible? Foreign Language
Annals 14(2):133-37.

Yes. Meaningful practice--a drill that cannot
be accomplished by a student unless the meaning
of the items is understood--is contrasted with
structural practice, where only structural
knowledge is essential and meaning is optional.
Structural drills involve, for instance, completing a sentence by providing the correct form
of a verb in parentheses; meaningful drills
involve choosing the appropriate verb from a
list and then providing the correct form.
Students using computerized exercises perform
better when the exercises are meaningful than
when they are simply structural. Meaningful
practice is not dependent upon interaction
between people.

Scherr, Barry P. and Lawrence W. Robinson. 1980.
Creating Computer-Assisted Drills for Russian:
The Structure of the Data Base. Russian
Language Journal 34(118):21-36.

The database described is a system for classifying lexical items in Russian so that they can be
inflected under program control. This approach
provides a radical improvement in the
flexibility of courseware. A coding system was
devised that made necessary compromises between
linguistically sound classifications of lexical
material and practical needs of the computer.
Extremely helpful and detailed information is
supplied concerning the way nouns and verbs were
classified so that others, especially Russian
instructors, can benefit from the insights
gained in the project. Since the program is
used as a supplement to instruction, an
elaborate instructional apparatus with a more
thorough analysis of errors is of secondary
importance.

Schneider, Edward W. and Julius L. Bennion. 1983.
    Veni, Vidi, Vici, via Videodisc: A Simulator
    for Instructional Conversations. System
    11(1):41-46.

    Explains the use of microcomputers with
    videodiscs to create authentic listening
    activities through simulated environments. Out-
    lining the production and format of
    "Montevidisco," the authors give a succinct but
    detailed view of what can become a major use of
    foreign language instructional technology.
    Students use a computer-controlled videodisc to
    interact with moving pictures filmed in a town
    in Mexico. Natives of the town address the
    student in Spanish and wait for an answer. What
    happens next depends on which of several alter-
    native answers the student chooses to give. By
    making suitable choices, a student can visit the
    market, a bullfight, a restaurant, a hotel, the
    hospital, etc. The urge to explore the town
    motivates several hours of listening and
    speaking.

Scott, Brian. 1983. Today's "Future" Technology for
    Language Study, Voice Recognition, and Word
    Verification. In Foreign Language Instructional
    Technology Conference Proceedings, 21-24
    September, 1982. Monterey, CA: Defense
    Language Institute. ED 236 910.

    Given the current state of speech recognition
    technology, the advantages of single-word
    verification are great: improved accuracy,
    faster response time, and extended vocabulary.
    The use of a voice-based instructional system
    for foreign languages is described.

Sherwood, Bruce. 1981. Speech Synthesis Applied to
    Language Teaching. Studies in Language Learning
    3(1):171-81.

    Describes the machinery, the process, and some
    pedagogic uses of synthesizing speech by means

of the PLATO system.  Esperanto is used as the
example:  given the imperfections of current
technology, any natural language would be objec-
tionably distorted by the process.  The author
types in material using a special command, and
the synthesizer scans the text and transforms
each letter into a numerical program that will
produce the appropriate sound.  A subroutine
counts the vowels in each word in order to place
the accent on the correct vowel, and that stress
is also counted with other word stresses to
create sentence intonation.  Commas produce a
pause.  Students identify words or pictures with
the synthesized speech they hear.  An error can
be made to generate a synthesized response:
"Not sanus, sonis."  That capability shows one
advantage of synthesized speech over a computer-
controlled audio tape player.  Other advantages
include the ease with which synthesized
statements are created, altered, and accessed.
A random-access disk audio device does allow
instantaneous access to any fractional second of
a twenty-minute disk, but synthesis is still
easier to create and alter on the PLATO system.

Stevens, Vance.  1983.  A Report of a Project
Illustrating the Feasibility of Video/Computer
Interface for Use in ESL.  CALICO Journal
1(1):27-30, 50.

Provides a description, a critical perspective,
examples, and a rationale for the use of
interactive video language lessons, in which a
video cassette recorder is connected to a
microcomputer to support listening comprehension.  The article contains a good deal of
information and practical advice, pointing out
some of the difficulties involved.  The video
tape medium may not be practical for use with a
computer; videodiscs seem to promise fewer
problems.

Taylor, Heimtraut (Heimy) F. 1979. Students' Reactions to Computer Assisted Instruction in German. Foreign Language Annals 12(4):289-91.

Describes existing computer programs that are used to supplement classroom and individualized instruction. Students react favorably to supplementary CAI tutorials on German grammar. Results from a questionnaire reflected a direct correlation between time and effort spent with the computer and level of satisfaction. The questionnaire helped the authors determine and remedy problems with unfamiliar vocabulary and with an unpopular requirement that students finish a particular segment with a specific number of correct answers before being allowed to move to another section.

Toong, Hoo-min D. and Amar Gupta. 1982. Personal Computers. Scientific American 247(6):86-107.

A thorough introduction, with diagrams, to the parts and processes of the personal computer.

Tuttle, Harry Grover. 1983. Programming/Evaluating Second Language CAI. Foreign Language Annals 16(1):35-39.

Gives some practical advice and guidelines on writing in BASIC and evaluating programs in foreign language CAI. The article illustrates the importance of clear and well-formatted titles and instructions; discusses planning for "non-educational errors," such as extra spaces; and emphasizes the importance and variety of appropriate feedback, including remediation and scorekeeping. Students must be given personal control over programs.

Underwood, John. 1982. Simulated Conversation as a
CAI Strategy. Foreign Language Annals
15(3):209-12.

Describes FAMILIA, a Spanish program written in
LISP, which simulates a (written) conversation
with the student at a terminal. It uses the
vocabulary of the family and the verbs ser and
estar to generate, accept, and comment on
student sentences. The program initiates and
continues the conversation by asking questions
about the student's family members: where they
are from; where they are now; what their professions are. FAMILIA identifies certain ungrammatical sequences by scanning for key words,
such as de used with estar, and points out the
rule, with an example, to help the student come
up with a better sentence. The program also has
a glossary function. When the student's Spanish
gets too badly garbled for the program to sort
out, it will respond with something like No
entiendo. This article points to one of the
major directions we can take in making the
computer engage in free and creative language
use with students.

Van Campen, Joseph. 1981. A Computer-Assisted
Course in Russian. In University Level
Computer-Assisted Instruction at Stanford:
1968-1980, Patrick Suppes, ed. Stanford:
Institute for Mathematical Studies in the Social
Sciences, Stanford University.

Describes a computer-assisted course in Russian
that relied solely on the computer to relay
information to the student. Extensive data are
presented on student performance. For translation of English sentences into Russian, CAI is
probably more effective than a regular
classroom-taught course. Samples of lesson
programming are provided.

Weible, David M. 1980. Teaching Reading Skills through Linguistic Redundancy. *Foreign Language Annals* 13(6):487-93.

Describes a contextualized vocabulary program in which the context supplied to help learners infer meanings is given in the native language. Students follow a sequence of sixteen English texts, with German words and structures replacing some of the English; drills are done on the German. The first text is 69 percent English and the last text is only 12 percent English. A study comparing results with students who did not use the computer suggests that the computer contributed significantly to learning.

Weible, David M. 1983. The Foreign Language Teacher as Courseware Author. *CALICO Journal* 1(1):62-64.

A well-argued appeal to foreign language teachers to try their hand at instructional programming through the use of an authoring system such as PILOT, PASS, or PROF.

Weischedel, Ralph M., Wilfried M. Woge, and Mark James. 1978. An Artificial Intelligence Approach to Language Instruction. *Artificial Intelligence* 10(3):225-40.

Using advanced programming techniques to store the syntax of both good and bad sentences, this project indicates possible directions for serious advances in foreign language CAI. The computer serves as a tool to assist students in developing reading comprehension and writing skills. In response to questions based on a text, students create full-sentence answers to a set of questions. The program uses its model of German to diagnose inappropriate use of vocabulary, misplaced words, well-formed answers that do not answer the question, and spelling errors. The prototype has been implemented for two texts and a vocabulary of 200 words. This

is one of the few articles available on the use
of artificial intelligence strategies for
foreign language instruction. A useful list of
references for this area is provided.

Winograd, Terry. 1983. Language as a Cognitive
Process. Volume 1: Syntax. Reading, MA:
Addison-Wesley.

A state-of-the-art guide for people who are
building computer systems that deal with natural
language. It describes relevant techniques in
detail and provides extensive references to
research in both linguistics and computer
science. Essential reading for those attempting
to escape canned drill.

Wyatt, David H. 1983a. Computer-Assisted Language
Instruction: Present State and Future
Prospects. System 11(1):3-11.

This state-of-the-art article introduces a
special issue of System devoted to computer-
assisted language instruction. The article
discusses reactions to CAI, hardware,
ready-to-use courseware (or packages), authoring
courseware, advanced technology (videodiscs,
random-access audio devices), and directions for
development. The perspectives are broad and the
advice is good.

Wyatt, David H. 1983b. Teaching the Receptive
Skills. In Foreign Language Instructional
Technology Conference Proceedings, 21-24
September, 1982. Monterey, CA: Defense
Language Institute. ED 236 910.

Attention is called to the potential benefits of
computer technology in teaching reading and
listening. Reading courses are based on syl-
labuses that include practical reading
strategies such as skimming and context guessing; general discourse features, such as pronoun
reference; and specific language features, such

as cause-and-effect or classification and
definition. Specific ways in which computerized
lessons can individualize the learning of these
skills are described. For computer-assisted
instruction to be feasible with this type of
reading skills material, all the evidence seems
to indicate that a very basic CAI system is
quite adequate. Similar observations apply to
the listening skills, but more elaborate audio
and video technology will be required.

Wyatt, David H. 1984. Computer-Assisted Learning in
English as a Second Language. Washington, D.C.:
CAL-ERIC/CLL; New York: HBJ International.


A general introduction to CAI in language
teaching with a focus on practical techniques
for ESL. Within various areas of language
instruction, activities are identified and
placed along a continuum ranging from the
mechanical, through the meaningful, to the communicative. Future directions and developments
are discussed; an appendix lists sources of
software and further information.

# Glossary

The borderline between jargon and useful terminology is fuzzy. While teachers can try to avoid the ubiquitous "inputs" and "interfaces" in their own speech, the materials they encounter will seldom be so circumspect. To help our readers penetrate the lexical jungle of instructional technology, we include the following glossary of terms we find useful, defined as straightforwardly as we can manage.

**Answer processing:** the way an instructional computer program handles students' answers; ranges from no evaluation, through a right/wrong judgment, to elaborate scanning for correct and incorrect segments; also known as **answer evaluation, answer judging,** or **response judging;** an **answer processor** is a computer program or routine for undertaking answer processing.

**Anticipated wrong answer:** a likely error stored for use by a computer program to help diagnose student answers, usually in drill or tutorial.

**Artificial intelligence:** qualities of a computer program that resemble human intelligence: the ability to learn from experience, to reason, to adapt, and to handle relatively unpredictable natural language.

**Associated pair:** paired words, translations, synonyms, antonyms, and the like, set up for use

126

in drill, especially vocabulary programs, where nearly automatic association of the two elements is desired.

**Authoring language**: a streamlined programming language designed for the convenient creation of lessons for the computer; usually more flexible than authoring systems, which may require highly fixed patterns of information.

**Authoring system**: a program or set of programs designed to allow teachers to write a computer lesson without requiring them to learn how to write a program.

**BASIC**: Beginner's All-Purpose Symbolic Instruction Code; a programming language common to many kinds of computers; can be used to create interactive computer lessons.

**Branching**: skipping from one to another place in a lesson, usually on the basis of students' performance.

**CAI**: see **computer-assisted instruction**.

**Character set**: the letters, numbers, and other symbols used by a machine or program to display information; may include accents and other special characters required for languages; may be modifiable by changes in equipment or in program operation.

**Command**: instructions the user gives to a computer program, usually coded as a more or less mnemonic symbol: H for HELP; S for STOP, etc.

**Compatibility**: the ability of a computer to accept and process programs written on or for another computer.

**Computer literacy**: sufficient knowledge of the computer to use some existing software; awareness of some of the possibilities and limitations of computers.

**Computer-assisted instruction (CAI):** instruction involving the use of the computer, usually by means of a student-computer dialogue in which the student and the computer take turns providing information to each other, and in which that information affects the course of the interaction; also called **computer-based instruction, computer-enhanced learning,** or **computer-assisted learning.**

**Concatenate:** the process of putting together groups of characters to create a word or sentence.

**Courseware:** instructional computer programs.

**Database:** a systematically arranged body of information that can be manipulated, expanded, and examined with the help of a computer; this activity is known as **database management.**

**Diagnosis:** the attempt to pinpoint or explain errors made by students using an instructional program; on a larger scale, the attempt to evaluate students' overall knowledge of a topic and find specific weaknesses or flaws.

**Digitized speech:** speech that has been recorded and converted into numerical values for use by a computer program.

**Disk drive:** a device in a computer system by means of which information stored on a plastic diskette is transferred to the computer's memory, or vice versa; provides faster access to data than a cassette recorder.

**Diskette:** a thin, flexible, plastic disk used by microcomputers to store information (programs, files, etc.); also called a **floppy disk.**

**Documentation:** materials that describe the design

and use of computer programs; usually a combination of printed materials and information contained in a program.

**Dot matrix**: a relatively inexpensive way of printing by computer; characters are composed of tiny dots, which means that special symbols and images can also be printed.

**Drill and practice**: a type of instructional computing in which students work on individual items, practicing discrete points of language knowledge.

**Error anticipation**: a way of handling possible student errors by predicting specific likely wrong forms and linking them to helpful messages that lead students to the right answer.

**Error trapping**: a process in the design of programs that insures that they will run smoothly and cannot be interrupted inadvertently; also a way of handling undetected errors contained in the program itself as they arise.

**File**: a collection of data, such as lesson materials, stored under one heading for use by a computer program; on microcomputer systems, files are stored on diskettes.

**Flashcard program**: elementary vocabulary CAI where students match words with words, meanings, or visuals; usually implies simple right/wrong evaluation and fast pace.

**Foreign-language authoring system**: program designed to allow foreign language teachers to write fixed kinds of computer lessons without any programming skills; the teacher concentrates on creating the language material, while the system handles the drill format, answer processing, record keeping, etc.

**Format:** the presentation of text on the screen or on paper, including headings, margins, spacing, centering, page numbering, underlining, and so on; in some text editors, the raw text is processed through a program known as a **formatter**, which follows the writer's instructions for preparing the format.

**Formative evaluation:** step in the creation of a computer lesson in which a small number of students use the program and provide information on possible design changes.

**Frame:** the information on the screen at one time, usually organized in a coherent whole so that it can be understood and handled as a unit; a visual and logical step in a lesson.

**Game:** rule-based, competitive CAI activities, usually involving timing and/or visual display features, in which the player must acquire and/or manipulate knowledge to succeed.

**Generative exercise:** exercises consisting of sentences that a computer program creates based on rules and lexical material, rather than drawing them from stored, fixed lists.

**Gradebook package:** program that maintains a teacher's records on individual students and classes, keeping track of scores and computing averages to help the teacher arrive at grades and related course statistics.

**Graphics tablet:** a device that allows the user to draw images for storage and display by the computer.

**Hardware:** the primary physical components of a computer; the machine itself: main unit, keyboard, disk drive, screen, and optional elements such as printers; contrasted with software.

**Help command**: the means by which a student can ask for some sort of assistance to answer a question; help may be technical (e.g., how to type accents); it may give an example; it may present a grammatical rule; or it may give the answer directly.

**Instructional computing**: all uses of the computer to support the instructional process, including not only CAI but also bookkeeping and other chores associated with teaching.

**Item bank**: a set of items for a given exercise or test; items are chosen by a program and presented to the student on the basis of content, difficulty, etc.

**Letter-quality**: high-quality printing under computer control, usually contrasted with dot-matrix printing.

**LOGO**: a programming language oriented toward the construction of programs from simple concepts; lends itself both to beginners' exploration of the power of the computer, especially through image building, and to the design of advanced hierarchical structures and lists used in artificial intelligence approaches to natural language.

**Mainframe computer**: a computer of the most powerful sort in terms of memory, processing speed, and number of terminals used simultaneously by different users.

**Menu**: the list of alternative actions available to a computer user at a given point; by selecting one of the menu options, users choose the particular lesson or activity they want next; **menu-driven** programs are simple for novice users to handle because they need not memorize or look up their options; contrasted with command-oriented approaches, which require knowledge of subsequent valid commands to the computer.

**Microcomputer**: a small, desk-top computer that usually serves a single user; **microcomputing** refers to the whole array of activities based on microcomputers.

**Module**: a self-contained lesson from a set of lessons that may be used in any order to accommodate different curricula.

**Optimize**: in drill, the process of leading a student toward a set goal by recirculating items in some systematic fashion until they have been mastered.

**Package**: a commercially available program or set of programs and their accompanying printed materials.

**Parsing**: machine analysis of the structure of a command, sentence, or text issued by a human; the basis for more advanced techniques for handling natural language.

**Partial answer processing**: the technique of checking a student's answer by looking for predicted wrong segments that are associated with specific error messages.

**Pattern markup**: a diagnostic strategy used to indicate the location and nature of errors in a student's response, often without referring to specific knowledge about the natural language in question.

**Peripheral**: any device connected to the computer: disk drive, printer, tape recorder, random-access audio or video equipment, etc.

**Polling**: the process by which the computer obtains information (an answer, a request for an exercise, etc.) from a student.

**Pool**: groups of similar textual items available to a program; pools of elements can either be used directly or combined by program logic to form larger units, such as sentences; by random selection, a small pool of items can be made to produce a very large and ever-varying set of materials.

**Presentation**: the whole complex of techniques and questions related to the ways in which material reaches the student, including timing, visual design, aural stimuli; may be controlled by the program or by the student.

**Problem solving**: a type of CAI lesson in which the student learns to use computer resources to solve problems; some reading and writing strategies lend themselves to this type of design.

**Program**: a logical sequence of instructions that can be interpreted by the computer and that is usually stored for future retrieval and use; a **programming language** is the predefined set of possible instructions understood by the computer.

**Random-access**: the ability to store and retrieve data directly and rapidly without conducting a linear or sequential search through surrounding data; the data may be information in a file, slides, videotape, recorded speech, etc., but for this kind of retrieval they must be stored on a random-access medium, such as a videodisc or a diskette, or in the computer's immediate memory.

**Random-access audio recorder**: a device that uses a disk to store recorded sounds and allows rapid access to any one of those sounds when it is attached to a computer.

**Record keeping**: the maintenance of a file of data, usually numerical, on students' performance.

**Retire:** to take an item out of circulation in the lesson, usually because it has been mastered.

**RETURN key:** the key most frequently used to signal to the computer that a student's response is complete; delaying evaluation of responses until this key is pressed allows the student the chance to correct errors.

**Selective branching:** the process of deciding which of several alternate paths through lesson material is most appropriate to the current student, based on previous performance.

**Simulation:** the presentation by a computer program of a dynamic model that reveals information about or analogous to the real world; the user can usually add or alter variables to influence the working of the system and draw conclusions about it.

**Software:** computer programs; contrasted with the equipment or hardware.

**Software package:** commercially available program or programs and the accompanying printed instructions.

**String:** characters manipulated by a computer program; contrasted with numbers, which may be stored differently; a **string operation,** is a built-in procedure that allows a computer program to examine strings, concatenate them, take them apart, or alter them; **string handling** is the composite ability of a given programming language and machine to manipulate strings.

**Support:** the continuing assistance guaranteed by the author, manufacturer, or distributor of computer products; if products are not **supported,** purchasers and users run a greater risk of encountering problems that no one is able or willing to solve.

**Synthetic speech**: sounds generated on the basis of numerical code that derives not from real speech but from some other source such as the manipulation of machine-based phonemes.

**Template**: a fixed format into which lesson materials can be inserted without extensive knowledge of how to write programs.

**Text editor**: one or more computer programs that store, format, edit, manipulate, and print text.

**Text entry**: the process of putting text into the computer.

**Text file**: a piece of text named and stored on the computer for later use, usually by a program such as a text editor or a lesson; often contrasted with a program, since most text files are destined for human consumption, while programs are interpreted by the machine.

**Timesharing**: the use of a computer by more than one person at a time, preferably in such a way that each person has the sense of being the sole user.

**Turn-key**: a program or system that requires virtually no prior training or practice; when the computer is turned on, it works; a desirable feature in instructional computing.

**Tutorial**: a form of CAI that presents new information, often coupled with exercises and a program that keeps track of student progress and decides what to teach next based on that information.

**Video monitor**: a television-like device, usually without audio, used to display information; sometimes called a CRT (cathode-ray tube) or a VDU (video display unit).

**Videodisc**: a disk resembling a phonograph record

that stores video and audio material; images and
sound are of high quality and can easily be
controlled for playback from any desired point
on the disk.

# ABOUT THE AUTHORS

Geoffrey R. Hope (Ph.D., University of Pennsylvania) is associate professor of French and Italian and secondary education at the University of Iowa, where he trains teaching assistants, directs first-year French, supervises student teachers, and teaches courses in foreign-language teaching methods, elementary French, and French literature. He has published articles on language teaching and literature in various journals. His software package ELFE, a comprehensive set of computerized exercises on French grammar, will be published by CONDUIT.

Heimy F. Taylor (Ph.D., Washington University) is associate professor in the Department of German at the Ohio State University, where she directs undergraduate German language instruction and supervises the training program for graduate teaching associates. She is the coauthor of DECU and TUCO, which are comprehensive computer tutorial programs for German. She has published on computer-assisted instruction, FLES, and individualized instruction in Foreign Language Annals and Unterrichtspraxis, among other journals, and has contributed papers to the Central States Conference, the AATG annual meeting, and the Northeast Conference. She is also the coauthor of a recently published intermediate textbook for German conversation. Her areas of specialization are CAI, language teaching methodology, and German literature of the 19th century.

James P. Pusack (Ph.D., Indiana University) is associate professor and chair of the Department of German at the University of Iowa, where he supervises the training of teaching assistants and teaches courses in techniques of translation, intensive language, and German fiction. He has contributed articles, papers, and workshops on CAI and teaching methodology to various journals and conferences. His foreign language CAI authoring system DASHER, An

*Answer Processor for Language Study*, was published by CONDUIT, where he now serves as language series editor. He also served as guest editor for a special issue (Spring, 1984) of *Unterrichtspraxis* devoted to applications of technology to German language teaching.

# Language in Education: Theory and Practice

Please order books in the series by ISBN and title. Send your orders to:

Harcourt Brace Jovanovich International

Orlando, Florida 32887 U.S.A.

Below is a selected list of series titles:

Volume 1 (1977-78)

6. From the Community to the Classroom: Gathering Second - Language Speech Samples, by Barbara F. Freed.
   $3.95.          0-15-599069-1
7. Kinesics and Cross-Cultural Understanding, by Genelle G. Morain.
   $3.95.          0-15-599225-2
8. New Perspectives on Teaching Vocabulary, by Howard H. Keller.
   $3.95.          0-15-599101-9
9. Teacher Talk: Language in the Classroom, by Shirley B. Heath.
   $3.95.          0-15-599081-0
10. Language and Linguistics: Bases for a Curriculum, by Julia S. Falk.
    $3.95.          0-15-599063-2
11. Teaching Culture: Strategies and Techniques, by Robert C. Lafayette.
    $3.95.          0-15-599107-8
12. Personality and Second Language Learning, by Virginia D. Hodge.
    $3.95.          0-15-599083-7

Volume 2 (1978-79)

13. Games and Simulations in the Foreign
    Language Classroom, by Alice C. Omaggio.
    $8.50.        0-15-599248-1
14. Problems and Teaching Strategies in ESL
    Composition, by Ann Raimes.
    $3.95.        0-15-599056-X
16. Testing Oral Communication in the
    Foreign Language Classroom, by Walter H.
    Bartz.       $.3.95.        0-15-599005-5
17. Intensive Foreign Language Courses, by
    David P. Benseler and Renate A. Schulz.
    $6.75.        0-15-599009-8
18. Evaluating a Second Language Program,
    by Gilbert A. Jarvis and Shirley J.
    Adams.       $3.95.        0-15-599089-6
19. Reading a Second Language, by G. Truett
    Cates and Janet K. Swaffar.
    $3.95.        0-15-599045-4


Volume 3 (1979-80)

25. ACTFL 1979: Abstracts of Presented
    Papers.      $5.95.        0-15-599001-2
28. Teaching a Second Language: A Guide for
    the Student Teacher, by Constance K.
    Knop.        $5.95.        0-15-599102-7
29. Assessing Study Abroad Programs for
    Secondary School Students, by Helene Z.
    Loew.        $3.95.        0-15-599111-6
30. Chinese Language Study in American
    Higher Education: State of the Art, by
    Peter A. Eddy, James J. Wrenn, and
    Sophia A. Behrens.        $5.95.
    0-15-599060-8
31. Sentence Combining in Second Language
    Instruction, by Thomas C. Cooper,
    Genelle Morain, and Theodore Kalivoda.
    $6.95.        0-15-599053-5

32. Teaching the Metric System in the Foreign Language Classroom, by Bette LeFeber Stevens. $6.95. 0-15-599271-6

Volume 4 (1980-81)

33. Directory of Foreign Language Service Organizations: 2, by Sophia A. Behrens. $5.95. 0-15-599008-X
34. The Older Foreign Language Learner: A Challenge for Colleges and Universities, by Elizabeth G. Joiner. $6.00. 0-15-599099-3
36. Helping Learners Succeed: Activities for the Foreign Language Classroom, by Alice C. Omaggio. $7.50. 0-15-599249-X
37. Discourse Analysis and Second Language Teaching, by Claire J. Kramsch. $19.95. 0-15-599103-5
38. Teaching Conversation Skills in ESL, by Ronald D. Eckard and Mary Ann Kearney. $3.95. 0-15-599059-4
39. Teaching French as a Multicultural Language: The French-Speaking World Outside of Europe, by John D. Ogden. $5.95. 0-15-559246-5
40. PR Prototypes: A Guidebook for Promoting Foreign Language Study to the Public, by Rosanne G. Royer and Lester W. McKim. $9.50. 0-15-599262-7

Volume 5 (1981-82)

43. Teaching Writing in the Foreign Language Curriculum, by Claire Gaudiani. $19.95. 0-15-599072-1
44. Functional-Notional Concepts: Adapting the FL Textbook, by Gail Guntermann and June K. Phillips. $6.00. 0-15-599078-0

47. Children's Second Language Learning, by
Barry McLaughlin. $7.00.
0-15-599223-6
48. Creative Activities for the Second
Language Classroom, by Diane W.
Birckbichler. $8.95.
0-15-599013-6
50. Error Correction Techniques for the FL
Classroom, by Joel C. Walz.
$5.75. 0-15-599286-4


Volume 6 (1982-83)

51. Language Variation and the ESL
Curriculum, by Miriam R. Eisenstein.
$5.95. 0-15-599061-6
52. Proficiency-Oriented Classroom Testing,
by Alice C. Omaggio. $9.95.
0-15-599250-3
53. A Guide to Language Camps in the U.S.:
2, by Lois Vines. $7.50.
0-15-599284-8
54. Hearing-Impaired Children in Regular
Classrooms, by Peter M. Blackwell.
$3.95. 0-15-599014-4


Volume 7 (1983 - 84)

56. Computers and ESL, by David H. Wyatt.
0-15-599297-X $7.95
57. Using Computers in Teaching Foreign
Languages, by Geoffrey R. Hope, Heimy
F. Taylor, and James P. Pusack.
0-15-599306-2 $7.95
58. Training Translators and Conference
Interpreters, by Wilhelm K. Weber.
0-15-599299-6 $8.95
59. Listening and Language Learning in ESL:
Developing Self-Study Activities for
Listening Comprehension, by Joan Morley.
0-15-599298-8 $6.95